11⁵⁰/1

S

Motivation Through the Work Itself

Motivation
Through the Work Itself

Robert N. Ford

American Management Association, Inc.

To
Professor Frederick Herzberg,
humanist and psychologist,
Case Western Reserve University,
who stimulated our search
for a way to introduce motivators
into the "work itself."

Acknowledgments

MORE THAN 100 PERSONS COOPERATED IN THE WORK-ITSELF studies. To give credit, and still avoid a long list of names, is not easy. I have, therefore, decided merely to list the Bell System associated companies that conducted trials and to mention the persons at the headquarters of the American Telephone and Telegraph Company who were responsible for guidance.

Harold Dunkelman, William Dytrt, and I worked very closely during the series of 18 trials. A special note of gratitude is due them, along with a candid admission that I can no longer separate my thoughts from theirs.

American Telephone and Telegraph Company, Headquarters
    Harold W. Anthony, Traffic Department
    Howard F. Brown, Treasury Department
    Robert Curran, Comptroller's Department
    Harold Dunkelman, Personnel Relations Department
    Bruce H. Duffany, Personnel Relations Department
    William L. Dytrt, Commercial Department
    John Q. Francis, Engineering Department
    Malcolm B. Gillette, Treasury Department
    Ronald O. Hadley, Commercial Department
    Peter B. Howell, Traffic Department
    Sylvester J. Huse, Comptroller's Department
    A. Philip Luse, Comptroller's Department
    George J. Lyons, Commercial Department
    Gene Nagel, Plant Department
    Wallace M. Regets, Engineering Department

Charles B. Robertson, Engineering Department
James H. Rourke, Jr., Comptroller's Department
Robert R. Sterrett, Engineering Department
Richard Walsh, Traffic Department
Roy W. Walters, Personnel Relations Department
Gilbert A. Wetzel, Plant Department
Ronald E. Young, Personnel Relations Department

Associated Companies of the Bell System

New England Telephone and Telegraph Company	— (2 projects, Commercial)
Southern Bell Telephone and Telegraph Company	— (1 project, Comptroller's)
Michigan Bell Telephone Company	— (2 projects, Engineering, Traffic)
Illinois Bell Telephone Company	— (4 projects, Plant, Commercial)
Northwestern Bell Telephone Company	— (1 project, Comptroller's)
The Pacific Telephone and Telegraph Company	— (2 projects, Plant, Comptroller's)
The Chesapeake and Potomac Telephone Company	— (2 projects, Commercial, Traffic)
AT&T, Long Lines Department	— (2 projects, Plant, Traffic)
AT&T, Treasury Department	— (Stock and Bond Division)
Bell Canada	— (2 projects, Commercial)

After the original study was conducted in 1965 with the correspondents in the Treasury Department of AT&T, the vice president and treasurer, J.J. Scanlon, established the first manpower utilization group with instructions to continue the work. Malcolm B. Gillette, who had directed the project, was placed in charge and remained director until 1968. He is now responsible for a similar group in Personnel Relations at AT&T headquarters, which is coordinating the manpower utilization effort throughout the Bell System.

A.S. Alston, now executive vice president of AT&T, was personnel vice president at the inception of the ideas under test in these trials. He and his successor, W.C. Mercer, have constantly supported the effort.

J.W. Kingsbury, assistant vice president, Personnel Relations, became particularly interested in this new area, offering not only his support but also ideas for analysis and presentation of data in certain sections which follow.

For a critical analysis of an early draft of this manuscript and for his encouragement toward completing the work, my thanks to P.C. Mabon, vice president of AT&T.

And for their critical but helpful comments, my thanks to the manpower utilization committee at the headquarters of AT&T in New York, to Jeanette Holobovich of Treasury, and to my wife, Jane. Finally, a note of thanks to Susan Cornell Werhner for her secretarial devotion in getting out this book.

ROBERT N. FORD

Contents

1

Introduction

THE PROBLEM THAT PRECIPITATED THE STUDIES IN THIS BOOK IS employee turnover. Since 1960 annual turnover rates involving many major jobs and virtually all departments in the Bell System have been mounting, as they have in many other American businesses. Exhibit 1 gives some typical data.

There is yet another turnover rate that many business people watch—the turnover among employees who have less than six months of service. This rate in any department is usually higher than those shown in Exhibit 1. This fact points up a particular problem: Employees who don't remain longer than six months are clearly expensive since they are not with the business long enough to return the costs of employment and training, especially if the job is complex.

THE OUTLOOK FOR REDUCED TURNOVER

In recent years, the U.S. job market has been a good one. Unemployment hit a 15-year low in November of 1968; according to the Bureau of Labor Statistics, only 3.3 percent of those in the job

Exhibit 1

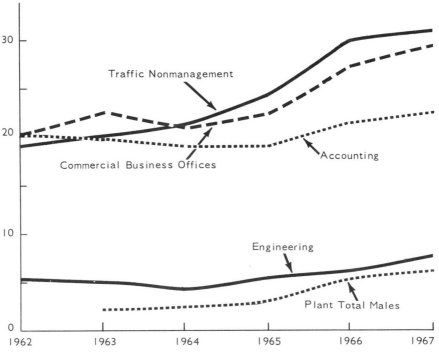

RESIGNATIONS AND DISMISSALS HIGHER (BELL SYSTEM)

Data exclude losses from death, retirement, leave of absence, and transfers between associated companies of the Bell System.

market could not find work. Obviously, there is a connection between the high employee turnover rate and a low national unemployment rate. When jobs are plentiful, a person does not have to keep an undesirable job; he simply leaves.

In some cities where the 19 studies in this volume were conducted, unemployment had dropped as low as 2 percent. Since many of the studies involved entrance-grade jobs to which young white collar workers—telephone operators, customer representatives, keypunch operators, and so on—are attracted, one can say that for all practical purposes there was no unemployment, because these jobs are of little interest to the unemployed: laborers, seasonal workers, building craftsmen, and others with established skills.

The market outlook for finding telephone operators and the

others easily in the future is quite dismal. Unless a business can learn to do a better job of holding the people it has, it had better learn to live with its current turnover rates.

When the top management of the Bell System reviewed the turnover data shown in Exhibit 1 for selected major jobs, one officer made the following comment about the unfavorable trends:

> We are going to have to make some changes in our thinking about the attitudes of young people today.

> We are told our potential employees are not motivated by fear of job security, for instance. We are going to have to appeal to them through having a reputation for providing jobs that allow a young person to make meaningful contributions in challenging work. Something is wrong, and we are going to have to look closely at our work, our measurements, our style of supervision. . . .

A WAY OUT

As early as 1961, examination of the problem and a knowledge of current research outside the Bell System led some of us in personnel relations to believe that the work itself might be the problem. The jobs, the actual tasks, were not quite right in some way. Employees were not motivated to perform the work itself.

Why not? Employees of the Bell System are reasonably well paid. A bargaining mechanism keeps wages in line with the market; job security is virtually unsurpassed; benefits are quite good.

The problem, we suspected, may be similar to that faced by a general who commands mercenary troops. Even though his opponents are ragged and unpaid, the general may have trouble if he is up against a band of patriots—people with a job to do and a commitment to do it. Even more formidable would be the *well-paid* band with a cause.

Let us drop this analogy quickly lest someone think the solution to industry's problem lies in patriotic films, slogans, songs, speeches, or any other form of exhortation. In fact, some suspect that this approach has already been done to death.

Instead, the solution attempted here in 19 trials was to improve jobs—the work itself—so that employees would naturally become more committed to the work and to the company. A "buy-off" was not to be the answer, although it may be a good solution for the short run. Turnover is not a short-range problem.

In fact, turnover rates do not fully measure the job problem. Lack of interest in one's work can show up in other ways, too. One of the personnel men in an associated company of the Bell System made the point neatly when he remarked in despair, "Our company has lost too many men who are still with us!" When employees are nearing retirement, or when they feel locked in their job situation for family or other reasons, the work itself is likely to be the only powerful motivator left. (If it is unrewarding psychologically, the employee is not up to standard regardless of wages. Turnover is not a sensitive measure of this, but there are other indicators—restricted productivity, excessive absenteeism, grievances, and so on.)

Surely the importance of work itself as a motivator is not startlingly new. On the other hand, not very much has been done in the way of systematically exploring methods of improving this work.

A Bit of Background

Our job enrichment trials, which began in 1964, grew out of good-natured bantering between the college recruiters and some of the employers of college graduates, notably those in the Treasury Department of the American Telephone and Telegraph Company. Turnover was sufficiently high to displease everyone. Tape recordings of exit interviews led to such remarks from the recruiters as, "You don't deserve the people we send you!"

The rejoinder was, "Then help us out. What should we do to hold the people you send us?" The trial, which is reported in Chapter 2, began in a spirit of high cooperation. Robert Ford was the consultant and report writer from Personnel; Malcolm Gillette was the study director from Treasury—the one who saw the project through after it had been assigned by the personnel head for the department, Howard Brown. We republish the paper here just as it appeared internally.

The results were so good that we decided to run a series of experimental studies on a number of other jobs. In this way we

Exhibit 2

OPERATING COMPANIES OF THE BELL SYSTEM

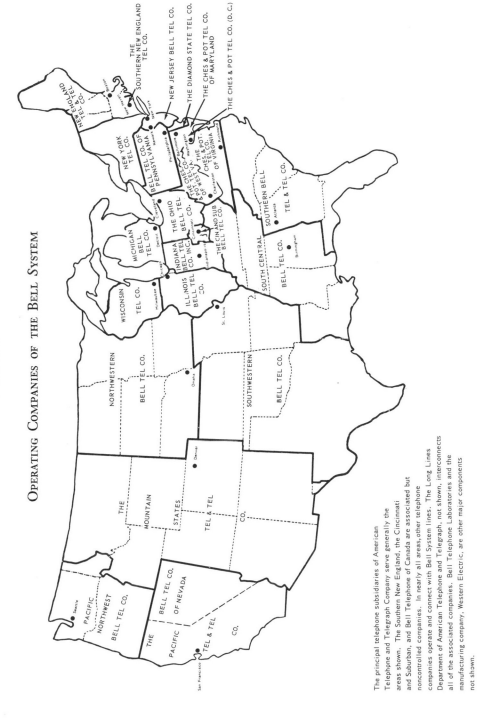

The principal telephone subsidiaries of American
Telephone and Telegraph Company serve generally the
areas shown. The Southern New England, the Cincinnati
and Suburban, and Bell Telephone of Canada are associated but
noncontrolled companies. In nearly all areas, other telephone
companies operate and connect with Bell System lines. The Long Lines
Department of American Telephone and Telegraph, not shown, interconnects
all of the associated companies. Bell Telephone Laboratories and the
manufacturing company, Western Electric, are other major components
not shown.

hoped to provide a basis for generalizing to the hundreds of jobs in the many departments of our vast public utility. The Bell System, of which AT&T is the parent company, employs more than 860,000 people in a group of associated companies extending from coast to coast, including Bell Telephone of Canada. The map (Exhibit 2) shows the operating companies. Studies were not made in the manufacturing company, Western Electric, or in the Bell Telephone Laboratories.

Eighteen replications of the original study are summarized in Chapter 3. As used here, "replication" means the studies were reasonably similar in fundamental thinking, study design, training sessions for supervisors, and time span. Although other trials are still in progress and much is yet to be learned, we have decided to publish this report because of many requests for information or for help inside as well as outside the Bell System. What is particularly striking is the great eagerness of managers to join in this effort whether they be from airlines, department stores, railroads, or the oil industry. Interestingly, requests for information have come from several branches of government, from public school administrators, from medical people, and from representatives of the ministry.

PURPOSE OF THE BOOK

If the studies reported here are accurate and the implications are fairly drawn, the framework for thinking about the tasks we give other people to perform should be of general importance. That framework and the results of experimentation are presented in a style that is intended to appeal to managers. In this context, a manager is anyone who assigns work to others, be he inside or outside a business.

Men who are laying plans and designing machines for the future should be interested also, unless no human beings will have to tend the machines in any way. One study included in these findings dealt exclusively with a new, highly sophisticated computerized billing arrangement. Much was accomplished by rearranging the related tasks so that a senior clerk could build a significant relationship to her work, rather than act merely as an adjunct of the machine, doing what it could not do.

The manager who tentatively accepts the finding that the tide of turnover can be reversed and who wants to move out on his own will find the details for doing so in Chapters 7 and 8. Thus the book contains a framework for considering the problem of work motivation, some studies and results, and a how-to-do-it section.

* * *

Since this application of social science to a business problem is in an incomplete state, the Bell System as an institution should not be asked or expected to *officially* endorse either the approach or the particular language used in this presentation. The author willingly assumes the responsibility himself.

2

Studies in AT&T's Treasury Department

PART A OF THIS CHAPTER CONTAINS THE REPORT OF THE ORIGINAL 1965 trial in the Treasury Department of AT&T. There are three reasons for including it:

1. By presenting it separately just as it was circulated in AT&T in 1966, the study may be judged on its own merits. It stirred up lively interest within the Bell System, and many people hoped the results were accurate. Getting others to cooperate in repeating the trial on different groups of employees was no problem. We asked for six more trials and easily got eighteen new ones started.

2. The report led to a departmentwide effort in Treasury, where there are about 1,200 employees in various jobs. Part B contains some new results. This is the only ongoing effort that can be published just now, and it is best understood in relation to the original study.

3. Three years later, the original trial still can be regarded as a

good effort. Better procedures have been developed (see Chapters 7 and 8); but, by beginning with the original study and then proceeding to newer trials, we can illustrate growth and change rather than simply present 19 identical studies, each a precise replication save for job, place, and employees.

The employees discussed in the following section are those who reply to inquiries from shareholders of AT&T. They all work in New York City.

A New Approach to Job Motivation: Improving the Work Itself

Robert N. Ford and Malcolm B. Gillette

SINCE THE START OF WORLD WAR II, BUSINESS MANAGEMENT HAS made unprecedented attempts to deal more successfully with the problem of work motivators and their effect on employee performance and attitudes. Because of questionable results from these many attempts, attention is now being directed toward a reappraisal of the total problem. In the pilot study reported here,[1] the striking results suggest that large gains can arise from the proper utilization of people on jobs, a direction that is quite tangential to the dominant themes of personnel administration during the past 25 years.

SOME MAJOR APPROACHES SINCE 1940

The labor shortages and high costs of World War II precipitated many ingenious responses to the need for more productivity, better quality, lower turnover, reduced costs, and better employee morale. All the major trends during the period from 1940 to 1965 were aimed at making the employee feel better about his job or about the company, with the hope that he would then improve his work. These trends included the following:

- Reduced hours and longer vacations.
- Increasing wages.
- Benefit packages.
- Profit sharing.
- Off-hours programs.
- Better training of supervisors in:
  - Human relations skills.
  - Sensitivity toward others.
  - Art of leadership.
  - Work analysis, planning, and control.
- Employee communication:
  - One way (company magazines, booklets, movies).
  - Two way (attitude surveys, discussion groups).
- Employee counseling service.
- Job participation.
- Organizational planning.

One thing is clear: In the 25-year effort to motivate employees along these lines, a satisfactory and lasting solution has not been

---

[1]The actual name and location of this work group and its immediate supervisor are not given lest we call undue attention to them. Their help is appreciated, of course, as are the cooperation and suggestions from G. N. Armstrong, assistant treasurer of American Telephone and Telegraph Company, and his operating staff, R. Tharaud, H. H. Chapman, Jr., P. A. Gratton, and K. G. Gruber.

found despite the efforts of many concerned and intelligent supervisors. Perhaps these efforts were necessary to maintain current productivity levels. Certainly, any employer who falls behind in such efforts will find himself in trouble; there is now a minimum threshold of job acceptability, vague but real.

The cold fact is that the vast and lasting gains in productivity have come from another approach to work—the kind of thinking that results in machinery and then automation, itself a new concept of this quarter-century. A cynic might say that the way to get more and better work done is to eliminate the worker. However, there is currently a great demand for workers, especially those who fill jobs that demand high intelligence. But workers often seem quite indifferent; they are said to be "unmotivated," and the previously listed approaches to motivation have not solved the problem.

THE NEW CONCEPT OF WORK MOTIVATION

The test case reported here, in which both quality of service and employee attitudes improved dramatically, stemmed from the thinking and observations of Professor Frederick Herzberg, a psychologist at Case Western Reserve University. In a review of the literature of job satisfaction studies, completed in the mid-1950's,[2] he and his co-workers reported perplexity. They then developed a theory that job satisfaction and dissatisfaction are not simple opposites: They may arise from different sources.

A depth-interviewing project followed, which has been replicated many times since 1959, in which employees talked about periods at work when they felt exceptionally good or exceptionally bad. The results, reported in *The Motivation to Work*[3] and in *Work and the Nature of Man*,[4] supported his hypothesis:

· Feelings of strong job satisfaction come principally from the task itself. The work motivators are

[2]Frederick Herzberg, B. Mausner, R. O. Peterson, and Dora F. Capwell, *Job Attitudes: Review of Research and Opinion*, Psychological Services of Pittsburgh, 1957.
[3]Frederick Herzberg, B. Mausner, and B. Snyderman, *The Motivation to Work*, John Wiley & Sons, Inc., New York, 1959.
[4]Frederick Herzberg, *Work and the Nature of Man*, World Publishing Company, Cleveland, 1966.

- The actual achievements of the employee.
- The recognition he got for the achievement (not to be confused with recognition as a human relations gesture).
- Increased responsibility because of performance.
- Opportunity to grow in knowledge and capability at the task.
- Chance for advancement.
- Feelings of dissatisfaction are more likely to be attached to the context or surroundings of the job, from the maintenance factors of
  - Company policies and administration.
  - Supervision, whether technical or interpersonal.
  - Working conditions.
  - Salaries, wages, benefits (salary sometimes serves as an indictator of success, but usually it was found among the dissatisfiers).

These maintenance factors are often called hygiene factors. In either case, the phrase connotes the importance of *preventing* trouble rather than *eliminating* it.

If Herzberg and his co-workers are right, the efforts of the past 25 years could not meet the employee's peculiarly *human* needs, for they were aimed at removing the causes of dissatisfaction by:

- Improving supervision and leadership.
- Improving such maintenance items as money, benefits, off-hours programs, and tuition aid.
- Improving company policies and administration.

This leads to the key notion: Removing these causes of dissatisfaction *will not* make people like their tasks. If one's task is boring prior to any of the changes just listed, it is no less a boring task afterward. It may be easier to tolerate in the short run, but it still lacks the essential ingredient: a long-range satisfier. To give a man that we must give him the work motivators; that is, give him a chance for

- Achievement (as he sees it, not as we do).
- Recognition associated with an achievement.
- More responsibility.

- Advancement to a higher order of task.
- Growth in competence.

These are long-range satisfiers, as shown in the motivator-maintenance theory and in 30 or more replications or variations of the original study.[5]

ON MOTIVATING PEOPLE TO WORK

The theory is quite clear on one point: You can't motivate workers from outside for long. But you can give them a chance to succeed and to improve at tasks that challenge them. Then they will develop their own drives toward tasks. These are the pertinent suggestions developed from Herzberg's position.

- Load the task with these true work motivators.
- Remove the dissatisfiers—the bad maintenance items (poor policies, poor supervision, poor wages, or anything around the task that blocks or annoys).
- Don't expect good maintenance items to make up for boring jobs. Think about them separately just as you do the parts of a football contest. The field, the stands, the crowd are not parts of the game itself. On the other hand, there will be no game without a field, at least.

Upon first encounter, many readers infer that the maintenance-motivation theory depreciates or denies the importance of the "field." If it does, it does not mean to. The theory is sharply calling attention to the importance of task motivation—the game—itself. When a human being has experienced the sweet joys of success (achievement, recognition, growth, advancement, and larger responsibility), he will move again, on his own, should he smell in the wind another chance to succeed. These are the dynamics of *The Motivation to Work*. It is a new statement, not folk wisdom in the area of motivating people to work well. Folk wisdom is better summarized by the quip, "Money may not be everything, but it's far ahead of whatever is in second place."

[5]*Ibid.*

The case that is presented here is this: Men work to meet their basic, *animal* needs. When they do, money is the medium. But money is not enough to satisfy *human* needs. With two-thirds of the 20th century and the days of terrible economic depressions behind us, we see that man is increasingly concerned with meeting these human needs—to achieve and to grow psychologically. If he cannot do so in the job he now holds, he will go elsewhere if possible; in any case, the maintenance items will be much the same wherever he goes. If he feels he cannot leave, he will tend to become a ward of the company with the company as his custodian until retirement or death does them part. The bargain is an uneasy one for both.

THE TEST SAMPLE

The study groups consisted of one group of 104 young women who answer customer complaint letters and another group of 16 girls who handle telephone calls from customers who phone rather than write. The problems raised and the information sought by the customers may be quite complex. The company therefore needs literate, intelligent girls; 70 percent of them are college graduates.

For many reasons the loss or turnover rate among these young women was high, and it was felt that something was not right. A decision was therefore reached to do something. But what?

Many changes could be made in the surround of the work, such as moving the operation to an attractive, convenient part of the city, paying more wages, changing the physical conditions around the work, and undertaking a communication program or perhaps an up-to-date general supervisory training course. In fact, there had been a number of steps to improve this aspect of the job.

With the Herzberg theory before us, we recognized that these approaches may have been dealing with the job dissatisfactions of these women. We elected this time to change *only the tasks* of the girls. The five objectives were to

1. Improve the quality of service (we have an index).
2. Maintain or perhaps improve productivity levels.
3. Improve the turnover situation.
4. Lower costs.
5. Improve employee satisfaction in job assignments.

The last item was assumed to be the key to the other four; improve deep job satisfaction, and the others would follow. This point of view was discussed with divisional top managers, and they encouraged us to develop and test the idea in their operations.

The girls were divided along natural supervisory lines into five groups:

1. *Achieving* group (20 girls). Their assignments were to be vertically loaded.
2. *Telephone* group (16 girls). The uncommitted supervisor of this group decided to make similar changes.
3. *Control* group (20 girls). The second-level supervisor was asked to ignore the study; nothing was said to the first-level supervisor or to employees.
4. *Uncommitted* group (19 girls). Nothing was said to first-level supervisors or to employees.
5. *Uncommitted* group (20 girls). As with the fourth group, nothing was said to the first-level supervisors or employees.

The volume of letters tapered off during the six-month study period, as expected, when a business problem was resolved. Therefore, some natural shrinkage in the size of the total group was allowed to occur: It decreased from 120 to 95. Of these girls in the September analysis, 90 were the same individuals who started out in March.

CLIMATE

SETTING THE CLIMATE—UPPER MANAGEMENT

The director for this project was thoroughly steeped in the philosophy of work as described previously. He worked with upper levels of management, telling them of the purpose of the study, and explaining that it involved a straightforward attempt to meet certain personnel problems through a new and relatively untested theory of work. He warned them of a possible initial drop in productivity and attitudes, but strongly encouraged them to make a demonstration effort. He asked for six months' tolerance and was granted it. Top managers did become anxious to stop the trial after five months, for an unusual reason: They could see real and current gains and wanted to install the changes in all the groups immediately. However, they were persuaded to let the trial run for the full six months, which had been estimated to be a reasonable minimum. It was assumed that, if initial results were poor (and they were!), the achieving group could perhaps work out the difficulty, given this much time. On the other hand, we wished to avoid being impressed by short-term gains, especially of the so-called Hawthorne effect type (that is, gains in productivity or attitude attributable to novelty or to the effect of being in the spotlight).

SETTING THE CLIMATE—SUPERVISORY LEVEL

In order to avoid the Hawthorne effect, the four first-level (immediate) supervisors of the young women in the planned achieving group *were not* called together, nor were the young women themselves told of the study. Instead, the project director met with the next higher level of management and talked about the importance of the work itself and about ways to improve jobs. He introduced the concept of loading a job vertically to improve it for the person performing it, as opposed to loading horizontally. Horizontal loading is simply enlarging a job or rearranging its parts without making it more challenging to the workers. Examples of rejected horizontal loading ideas applicable to the jobs of these girls include the following:

- Setting firm quotas of letters to be answered each day.
- Channeling all difficult, complex inquiries to a few women so that the remainder might attain high rates of output. These jobs could be exchanged from time to time.
- Rotating the girls through the telephone unit, to units handling different customers, and then back to their own units.
- Letting the girls type the letters themselves, as well as compose them, or take on such other clerical functions as reviewing the files or obtaining detailed information. (Indeed, this might really have been "unloading" the job for these bright young women.)

Obviously, this type of loading does not really improve the task. But it is unquestionably *aimed at* this end. We often turn completely away from a bad job assignment and attempt to make the work tolerable by improving rest rooms, adding soft music, subtracting time worked via coffee breaks, and so on. In effect, these moves say, "This work is boring, but it must be done. Please do it and we'll try to reduce the level of pain."

Job improvement assumes that the job probably does not have to be done as it is done now and that it can be made more challenging. Some ideas for consideration in the vertical loading of jobs are shown in the listing that follows.

Method of Loading	*Motivator Involved*
Removing some controls without removing accountability.	Responsibility and personal achievement.
Increasing the accountability of individuals for their own work.	Responsibility and recognition.
Giving a person a whole natural unit of work (module, exchange, district, division, area, and so on).	Responsibility, achievement, and recognition.
Job freedom; that is, giving additional authority to do or decide.	Responsibility, achievement, and recognition.
Making periodic reports directly available to the worker himself rather than to the supervisor.	Internal recognition.
Introducing new and more difficult tasks not previously handled.	Growth and learning.
Assigning specific or specialized tasks to individuals, helping them to become experts.	Responsibility, growth, and advancement.

With this list before them, the third- and fourth-level supervisors and the project director agreed that there were at least seven possibilities for change in the work being done.

1. Subject matter experts were appointed within each unit for other members of the unit to consult with before seeking

supervisory help. (Later on, it was found that the girls had rearranged these assignments among themselves along lines they felt to be more meaningful. This was a real test of the climate of responsibility we were trying to build, and it was accepted as such by management.)

2. Correspondents were told to sign their own names to letters from the very first day on the job after training. (They were simple letters, to be sure, but previously the verifier or supervisor usually signed for many months.)

3. The work of the more experienced correspondents was looked over less frequently by supervisors, and this was done at each correspondent's desk. Verification dropped from 100 percent to 10 percent. (This can be a source of significant dollar savings—$12,000 per group per year, if quality holds up, or more if it improves.)

4. Production was discussed, but only in general terms: "A full day's work is expected," for example. (As time went on, the supervisors said, it was not necessary even to mention production. *Less pressure* than usual is the direction of this change.)

5. Outgoing work went directly to the mail room without crossing the supervisor's desk. (Oddly enough, some experienced workers had trouble in breaking up this dependent relationship.)

6. All correspondents were told they would be held fully accountable for quality of work. (Prior to that, responsibility was shared with verifiers and supervisors.)

7. Correspondents were encouraged to answer letters in a more personalized way, avoiding the previous form-letter approach. (If a customer's letter is complicated, this can actually lead to better service and a higher quality index.)

One third-level supervisor discussed the proposed changes and the project with his second-level (group) supervisor and gave it his warm endorsement. They agreed on a plan to introduce the changes quietly at a rate of about one per week. As yet, there is no indication that the first-level supervisors or their people are aware that a special research study had been under way. The changes took place so naturally and were introduced so gradually by the group supervisor to her first-level supervisors, and by them to the girls, that they accepted the changes as normal routine.

This list does not include all feasible ideas, not even for this job. The third- and fourth-level supervisors reported that building the list was a challenging task for them. The list in turn became a challenging task for those persons whose jobs were being restructured. It is significant that these changes resulted from helping middle management to see the meaning of work as their employees see it. The knowledge was already present, but it was unorganized. No employee attitude surveys, job participation techniques, or consultants were used as sources of ideas for these changes since a better source was available—the supervisors themselves, many of whom had previously held jobs of the type they were now supervising.

SETTING THE CLIMATE—EMPLOYEE LEVEL

Here an effort was made to maintain the natural work situation. There were no important changes in wages, hours, policies, training, or the surround of any groups. No girl was transferred from the achieving group to any other. No new supervisors were added to the group during this period.

These groups of girls all worked on one floor of the same office building. The control group and the achieving group worked side by side, separated only by a five-foot partition. Any changes in desk arrangements or other physical conditions were made identically in all groups.

It is very important that none of the 14 first-level supervisors or their people was ever told that a study was in progress. Only the second-level supervisors of the achieving and control groups were told that a study was actually taking place, and they were told only because they had parts to play.

THE MEASURES OF SUCCESS OR FAILURE

Clearly, management wanted these workers to feel better about their jobs. To measure their feelings, a job-satisfaction questionnaire was constructed, composed of 16 items dealing exclusively with feelings toward the task (not toward any maintenance item). Questions in this "Reaction to Your Job" instrument cover chances for achievement on the present job, recognition for what is accomplished, breadth of responsibility, and chances for growth and advancement. Here are two sample questions:

> As you see it, how many opportunities do you feel you have in your job for making worthwhile contributions?
>
> 0 ☐ Almost none
> 1 ☐ Very few
> 2 ☐ A few
> 3 ☐ Quite a few
> 4 ☐ A great many
> 5 ☐ Unlimited
>
> Think about the specific duties of your job. How often have you felt unable to use your full capabilities in the performance of your job?
>
> 0 ☐ Almost always
> 1 ☐ Very often
> 2 ☐ Fairly often
> 3 ☐ Not very often
> 4 ☐ Very seldom
> 5 ☐ Almost never

The items are all scored 0 at the unfavorable end and 5 at the "good" end. The simple sum of the 16 items is the measure of job satisfaction used in this study, with possible scores ranging from the extremes of 0 to 80. In this instance the actual range is from 8 to 74. If the achieving group gained no more than did the control group, then the whole project would be deemed a failure.

The two formal work indexes, both of which were already in existence for these workers, cover quality of customer service and productivity. Management was especially hopeful that the quality of the customer service index might improve. This complex measure deals with such components as the correctness of the response to a customer's letter, the speed of response, and the accuracy of the details and any matters considered to be factual. The measure is prepared on a sampling basis, and the results are made available monthly for the groups, not for individuals.

Other measures cover changes in absenteeism, turnover, results of exit interviews (all of which were recorded on tape), movement upward into higher-level jobs, and such less tangible items as disciplinary incidents.

THE RESULTS—CUSTOMER SERVICE INDEX

As is made clear in Exhibit 3, all groups have shown an improvement in their indexes, with Groups I and II well ahead. Both statistically and from management's point of view, these are very good gains.

Exhibit 3

CUSTOMER SERVICE INDEX—A THREE-MONTH CUMULATIVE AVERAGE

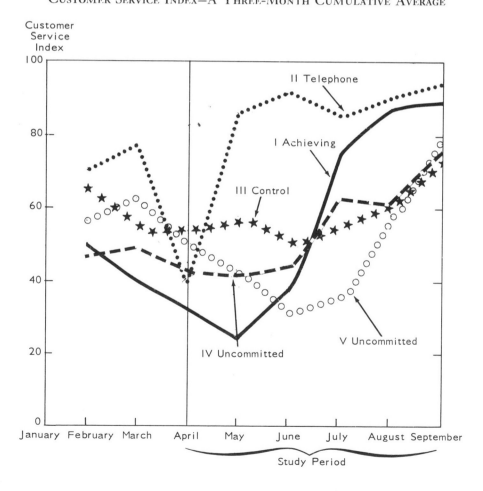

Group II, composed of girls who do not write letters but answer telephone inquiries, was not deliberately set up as an achieving group. The third-level manager of this group asked if he might load their jobs vertically too, since the achieving group (I) was also under his supervision and since the telephone group was not a formal control group. The project director acquiesced, but he did not deliberately help this group. The precise steps the third-level man took are similar to the seven outlined earlier, but are not identical and not as far reaching. There is one common ingredient; both Group I and Group II had their jobs loaded without any change in the surroundings of the job or in the maintenance items. Neither group knew that an experiment was going on.

The drop in the index from 33 to 27 by Group I tested management's commitment to the project, but it weathered the drop. The first two months were a period of readjustment for the girls, and the added responsibility was puzzling to them at first, although they later accepted it and approved it. They seriously questioned the accuracy of the index of 27 for the month of May rather than their own performance.

There are several reasons why Group II, the telephone group, improved faster. In the first place, the April dip in their service results is deceptively against the trend because of a peak period of work which occurs annually.

When this period was over, changes were introduced rapidly since the group was not either an achieving group or a control group. For all practical purposes, Group II's performance may be about the upper limit of what can be expected under ideal conditions. The nature of the job—telephoning, as contrasted with letter writing— may have helped here since the spontaneity of a telephone inquiry carries with it both immediate challenge and responsibility. Indeed, the changes made for the achieving group were intended to carry them in that direction.

OTHER QUANTITATIVE RESULTS

Turnover was greatly reduced during the period of the study. Only one girl resigned from the achieving unit. She did not like the added responsibility and felt that other employees should verify a correspondent's work. Turnover in the control group and in the two uncommitted groups continued at the former levels.

Absence control was constant before and during the project, since no big problem existed here. Even so, the frequency of long-duration absences declined, as well as the total frequency of incidental absence among the achieving workers, from 2.0 percent to 1.4 percent. The control group had a slight increase during these six months, from 2.0 percent to 2.3 percent.

Productivity is hard to measure since the composition of a truly correct reply to a letter can take from 20 minutes to 2 days, depending on the problems raised. Both Group I and Group II are *ahead* of their old levels, but this is not an important gain, nor was it a particular problem. To maintain the previous level was good enough.

Promotions are being made in larger proportions out of Groups I and II. The third-level supervisor and the project director agree that this is the product of the better performance of these groups. This performance gain is conspicuous enough that the higher levels of managers can identify it even in a six-month period. Conversely, the manager stated, "Now I know whom to drop! If they cannot do the job, if they cannot take the responsibility for producing a good letter of reply without the supervisory crutch, then we cannot carry them. Before, we did not really know who was competent because verifiers or supervisors checked everything, making sure that no one failed and seeing to it that errors were very low."

Cost reduction was not a major criterion of the study since it is difficult to separate the gains objectively. If these preliminary results continue to hold, then the expensive verification step can be reduced from 100 percent to 10 percent, turnover will probably drop, and training costs will go down. As noted earlier, management was sufficiently convinced of the gains that it could hardly wait to get all five groups onto the same basis. Some other cost findings will be mentioned later.

Offsetting the gains was the expense of the program—a quite limited sum, which was essentially part of the project director's salary. (He had many other duties.) This may prove to be one of the least expensive of all the personnel motivation efforts since 1940, in any net cost sense.

SOME SUBJECTIVE RESULTS

The supervisors in the project have volunteered these important observations or, rather, impressions of the project:

1. The achieving group members are talking more about their job responsibilities than about the maintenance items. They say that they feel pressure from *themselves* (a deep feeling of responsibility) to get the work out quickly and correctly.

2. The service check that goes into the customer-service index is fully accepted by the achieving group as a much-needed quality inspection device. Keen interest in accomplishment is shown by employee requests for *individual* service feedback. The girls tell their supervisors if a mistake has been discovered after the customer contact, and they immediately get in touch with the inquirer to correct the error. They have a pride in group achievement. Previously, the service index represented outside pressure rather than a means for knowing internally whether one is competent.

3. The girls report that their letters and telephone calls are more complete and relevant, thereby requiring fewer repeat letters and calls from these customers on the same problems. Supervisors state improved communication results in fewer "messes," which formerly took valuable time to straighten out. This time is now utilized by the groups to improve production rather than to correct errors.

4. Higher group morale is demonstrated by group enthusiasm toward work problems. (The theory did not predict this result; it did predict that each individual would like his work more.)

5. Two girls in the group who had been personnel problem cases have become valuable employees in this six-month period. Supervisors recently stated that they have not had any "small, annoying personnel problems" since May, whereas such problems had been almost a daily occurrence.

6. Supervisors are finding more time to analyze problems and to be available to their subordinates. They now say they feel as though they are managing the job instead of merely

verifying outgoing letters. The girls themselves now accept this responsibility and do the job completely on their own with the good results shown in Exhibit 3. This releases the supervisor for actual supervisory work (another intangible cost item).

How the Women View Their "New" Jobs

Spectacular work results can arise from a spectacular short-term motivator such as a special campaign that offers a prize or special reward. Such an offer actually was made, and one of the uncommitted groups not only checked, but double-checked most of the work. The customer-service index for this group did hit 90 for one month, but it dropped the next. The girls admitted later that they had not improved the *quality* of their work. This indicates that a rising index may or may not reveal a change in quality or satisfaction with one's work. Conceivably, there could be a negative relation; it is usually possible to raise indexes through supervisory pressure. How then, did these girls feel about their jobs in March as compared to September?

Using mean scores from the "Reactions to Your Job" questionnaire, Exhibit 4 shows the striking improvement in the achieving group's attitudes toward tasks as compared to the attitudes of the control group. In every one of the 16 questions, analysis showed that points were gained for a group average of almost 15. Meanwhile, the average of the control group dropped four points. There is less than one chance per thousand that this is merely a sampling fluctuation.

On this major criterion for the project—can we help employees to react favorably to the work?—the project is a success indeed. But the project director strongly believes that much ground can still be gained with the achieving group. He does not accept the end-of-project score as a theoretical maximum for this job.

The source of his belief is partly the questionnaire itself, which provided a place for spontaneous comments. In March many of the girls commented on the need "to show you what I can do!" In September this need had diminished a great deal in the achieving group, whereas it was as strong as ever in the control group. A

Exhibit 4

ATTITUDES TOWARD TASKS—CHANGE IN MEAN SCORES
OVER SIX-MONTH PERIOD

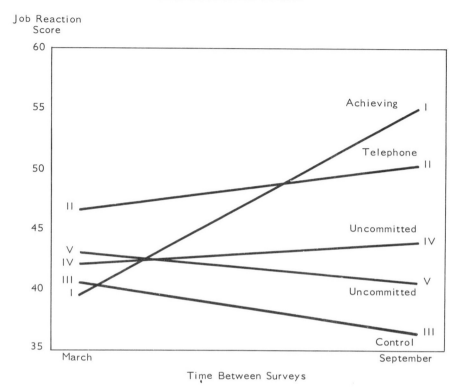

synthesis of the comments from the final survey of the achievers follows.

In brief, these are the things the achieving group members said at the time of its final survey:

- They now derive greater satisfaction from the job and feel that their performance has improved because of this.
- They now see more opportunity than they saw before and realize that opportunity now depends upon their own initiative and goals.
- The company still controls things too much and does not as yet fully recognize or appreciate the talent it hires and pays

for. Some want even more opportunities for achievement and more responsibility loaded into their jobs.

They find the job more interesting and now see more things to be learned. They spend most of their time now working out solutions to problems rather than wondering if the company will ever change the color of the office walls.

It may be that the better indexes in the control and the uncommitted groups have been achieved at a price the company does not want to pay. Exhibit 4 shows that the task attitudes of two of the three nonstudy groups are down a bit, even though Exhibit 3 showed their customer service indexes to be up. The work indexes can be maintained and perhaps improved through supervisory pressure and the expense of 100 percent verification of all letters. Needless to say, the company feels doubly repaid if it not only gains in its work indexes but meets the human needs of its employees.

SUMMARY

Herzberg's theory of work holds that the possibility for deep satisfaction with one's job lies in the task itself. The surroundings of the task can produce dissatisfactions, but not long-run satisfaction. Good policies, good administration, good wages and benefits, good supervision—all of these merely set the stage; they are not enough to hold capable humans to their jobs in a fluid job market.

The surroundings of the task were deliberately held constant while the tasks were improved for a group of women. They were provided greater chance for achievement, for recognition, for responsibility, for advancement, and for psychological challenge and growth.

The achieving or experimental group clearly exceeded the control and uncommitted groups on a variety of criteria, such as turnover, the quality of customer service, productivity, lowered costs, lower absence rates, and source for managerial upgrading. While the control and uncommitted groups also gained moderately on these indexes during the six months of the study, only the experimental group members felt significantly better about the task at which they work. The upward change in this group is most striking. Not all members of the achieving group moved upward and a few did not move very far. Thus there is still room for them to improve and there is still challenge for the managers.

This experimental study offers some confirmation for the idea that large gains can result from improvements in the work itself with little out-of-pocket expense, and it suggests a plan for achieving these gains.

CONCLUSIONS

This newer understanding of deep job satisfaction leads one to believe that the concepts of personnel utilization need rethinking today. Personnel utilization studies usually assume that certain jobs exist and that the problem is to man them with proper people both now and in the future as people resign or as the organization expands. This is a fairly static model.

The concept of manpower utilization in this study is more dynamic. Given an organization of people, what do we have them doing? The concept presumes that we often do not use people to their maximum—by either their standards or ours. Overhiring is only one reason; as a job becomes familiar (boring), the worker will seek challenge elsewhere if he can. The job is only a shadowy outline of what it might be, rather than a given fact. Thus, a challenging job for a man this year may not be so next year. Perhaps there are some jobs where loading with a chance for achievement, increased responsibility, and so on is impossible, but we suspect that most jobs can be loaded much more heavily than they are at present. If a job is deemed impossible after attempted loading, we must either automate the job or hire only those people who meet its minimum requirements. It is to be hoped that they will find a challenge in it.

Each leader's job is to provide tasks to his immediate subordinates which challenge them to the very limit of their abilities. How to help him do this is a nice problem for management trainers. Ready-made materials were not at hand for the three major parts of the job: (1) to focus management's attention on the problem, (2) to get management to believe that job improvement is worth undertaking, and (3) to do the job of improvement.

Organizational planning clearly follows vertical job improvement under this concept of work. Since loading jobs to the maximum takes time, job organization must be tentative until we see the outcome.

Regarding the panoply of benefits, the manner in which we deal with each other, the off-hours programs, and so on, let this be said: You've got to meet the market on these items. Once you have done that, turn instead to improving the tasks themselves for rewarding results.

Part B

Permanency of Results:
Treasury Revisited 18 Months Later

AT THE CONCLUSION OF THE TRIAL, TOP MANAGEMENT IN THE Treasury Department of AT&T set up a small manpower utilization group. Its responsibilities were to spread an understanding of work itself as a motivator and to help others get started, if they wished. As time passed, the members also became consultants on current and proposed jobs.

There were many people in many jobs to be reached eventually —more than 1,150 employees all told, of whom several hundred were supervisors. An even larger number, such as the shareholder correspondents and programmers, were specialists in nonsupervisory jobs. In this period, part of the organization was switching to a new computer system, and the entire organization was contemplating a move to a new location miles away. Such major changes do not necessarily make for improved job satisfaction! Quite the reverse can happen: Turnover can increase, productivity can drop, and service to shareholders can deteriorate.

The manpower utilization group carried on its indoctrination and educational effort through an 18-month period. Films, books, and articles were used; group meetings and individual meetings were held. A report concerning this group's philosophy of work and its particular approach in working with managers appears as Appendix A.

There is no reason at all for an improved job to stay improved after all the management force has been promoted or transferred to other jobs, as they were in Treasury. The achieving correspondents, too, were being rapidly promoted or rotated to give them wider experience, and inexperienced girls were taking their places.

The other groups of correspondents and their supervisors knew nothing of the study, and, therefore, nothing was happening to improve jobs in their groups. Clearly, job reshaping, as a means of improving manpower utilization, is not automatic. Merely reading the account of the trial in Part A of this chapter has not enabled others to go and do likewise.

But there is indeed a payoff for systematic effort. Without going into details here (see Appendix A for the procedures), let it be noted that the shareholder service index for all four corresponding groups (not merely the old achieving group) stays now in the upper 90's. (See Exhibit 5.) The Treasury study ended in late 1965. Results dropped in early 1966 from the high shown in Exhibit 3 during the time when the manpower utilization group was getting started under the direction of Malcolm Gillette. It had to reach not only the control and uncommitted groups but also the depleted achieving group.

The small manpower utilization team was working in other parts of Treasury's Stock and Bond Division also, wherever its offer of assistance was accepted. Exhibit 6 presents illustrations of what had been accomplished in late 1967, after 18 months. No effort has been made to make the list exhaustive, nor was it audited in any

Exhibit 5

COMMUNICATIONS SERVICE INDEX—ALL CORRESPONDENTS' UNITS
(THREE MONTHS' MOVING AVERAGE)

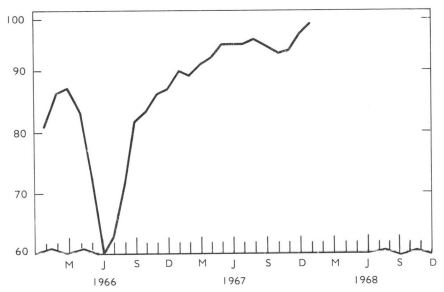

sense. Such an audit would be a misdirected effort because the data were not obtained under the scientific conditions of the original study, where there were both control and experimental groups. The figures in Exhibit 6 are known savings.

Perhaps some of these jobs would have been eliminated anyhow, and turnover would have dropped on its own. Three other examples, amounting to $90,000, could be added to the list in Exhibit 6. Suffice it to point out that large savings are possible in this job improvement effort.

We can lay aside the Treasury follow-up case, which is now a way of operating and not a project. It has served its purpose here if it now answers the question, "Can *permanent* gain result from a work-itself effort?" Apparently, the answer is yes.

Treasury Department officials went into this effort to make certain that every person in Treasury had as satisfying a job as could be created. They knew the consequences of bad jobs in terms of turnover, poor workmanship, and tension between bosses and employees as well as among employees themselves. Quite clearly, a

Exhibit 6

POSSIBLE SAVINGS, FIRST 18 MONTHS
AT&T TREASURY DEPARTMENT—STOCK AND BOND DIVISION

1. 27 percent drop, turnover, nonsupervisory specialists $245,000

2. Investigation and file clerks—salaries, annual 135,000
   - Force reduced from 46 to 24 clerks
   - Three management jobs eliminated

3. Correspondents' group—salaries 76,000
   - Five management, four verifier jobs eliminated

4. Stock transfer group—salaries eliminated 40,000

5. Merger of employee stock-pension unit and dividends
   reconciliation unit—salaries eliminated 100,000

6. Improved productivity (not priced) .... ?

7. Improved service indexes (not priced) .... ?

8. Improved tone of exit interviews (not priced) .... ?

9. Personnel section, job rearrangements (not priced) .... ?

10. Offset—half salary, six employees who work on this
    part-time .... (38,000)

     Total $558,000

work-itself effort is justified if it simply creates a personally satisfying place for its employees. For many years, the Bell System has held "good jobs" as one of its major goals along with good customer service and fair shareholder treatment.

If job improvement pays off handsomely and in unexpected ways —the pinpointing of jobs that are not needed and jobs that can be collapsed or dropped—so much the better.

Employers generally found that most post-World War II attempts to make jobs more satisfying became added business costs. The preliminary evidence from the work-itself effort in Treasury, however, strongly suggests that the costs are self-liquidating and then some.

3

Results of the Controlled Experiments

HAVING HAD A PREVIEW OF THE RESULTS IN ONE DEPARTMENT— Treasury—let us turn to the new series of controlled experiments elsewhere in the Bell System. Since the initial thinking, the procedural details, and the results have already been examined, what is presented here covers only conclusions and, where relevant, supporting data from the 18 new trials.

Chapter 4 presents a completely independent appraisal or audit of one project which has been quite successful. Chapters 5 through 8 present a distillation of all the reports—which run to hundreds of charts, tables, and pages—to provide the best interpretation of what was done in these studies and what should now be done.

So that one may get a reasonably close look at a project and a report other than the Treasury trial, the framemen trial has been included as Appendix B; this report will be most enlightening after Chapters 5 through 8 have been reviewed. From the framemen trial came many insights as to what goes wrong with a job after a time and many ideas for steps that could be taken to reconstitute the job.

WAS THE TREASURY TRIAL REPRESENTATIVE?

When the Treasury trial ended and the report was released, many readers said, in effect: "We believe your report. The test situation seems about as scientifically clean as one can find where real groups of people are involved. But *my* employees are different; they're not much like your college graduates. I wonder if it would be true for my men"—or my engineers or high school dropouts or whatever.

Such skepticism is legitimate, of course. Although the Treasury results might be viewed as reasonably representative of a universe of all Treasury correspondents in the statistical sampling sense, the results were most inadequate if viewed as a sample of employees in all Bell System jobs.

The similarity between the job of a correspondent and that of the typical service representative of the Commercial Department was fairly obvious. The service representative is the young woman who is contacted by a customer or prospective customer who has a service problem. With the help of the Commercial Department, eight such groups were studied and are reported upon in this chapter. With their controls, they total 3 percent of all Bell System service representatives. This might have been a fine sample had it been drawn strictly at random or in one of the other legitimate ways which permit formal tests of statistical significance. However, it wasn't. The eight districts and their controls were all urban, since that was where the problem of high turnover was centering.

Because no claim can be made for purity of statistical design in these operational studies, we will not press our scientific luck by making large claims for small differences. And, since we cannot honestly do so, we will not use formal statistical tests of significance based on *known* sampling structures.

On the other hand, the operating managers involved and the departmental staff consultants at AT&T headquarters consider some of the differences that follow overwhelmingly large. The judgment of whether a study is quite successful, modestly successful, or not successful is a consolidation of informed opinion in every case.

WHAT IS THE SAMPLING DESIGN?

The 19 studies in Exhibit 7 have a rough sampling outline even though no claim is made for scientific adequacy:

1. Six major departments of the telephone business are represented, as follows:

	No. Projects
Commercial	8
Comptroller's	3
Plant	3
Traffic	3
Engineering	1
Treasury (original)	1
Total	19

2. Each project group was an ongoing, working entity of the Bell System. Employees came and went, as did supervisors, although the request was made that movement of supervisors be strictly minimized. As might be expected, supervisors were transferred anyhow; some were hospitalized, and one died. But, if minimal movement had not been requested, there would probably have been somewhat more of a flow in the supervisory jobs of both the achieving and control groups.
3. Every project but one had a formal control group, which matched reasonably well. When a statement is made indicating an improvement, this always means "relative to the control data," save in the case of Virginia Traffic. There a program was used rather than a project in order to see how well the ideas would be accepted if they were made available to any supervisor. The control was the group's own past performance.
4. The employees involved (well over 1,000 each on the achieving and control sides, plus Virginia Traffic) are
   · Nonsupervisory, exclusively.
   · At 19 different locations in 10 companies.
   · Of both sexes.

(Text continues on page 50.)

Exhibit 7

Work-Itself Projects

Department	Job	Trial No.	Locations	Size of Achieving Group at Start of Trial
Treasury	Shareholder correspondent	1	New York City	28
Commercial	Service representative	2	Bell of Canada Toronto	50
		3	Montreal	75
		4	Illinois Bell Chicago	40
		5	Suburban—Office 1	25
		6	Suburban—Office 2	25
		7	New England Northern Massachusetts	70
		8	Rhode Island	60
		9	Chesapeake & Potomac Maryland	65
Traffic	Toll operator	10	Michigan Bell Saginaw	250
		11	AT&T—Long Lines Dept. New York City	350
Plant	Installer	12	Pacific T&T (Large Urban)	45

Department	Job	Trial No.	Locations	Size of Achieving Group at Start of Trial
		13	Illinois Bell Chicago	30
	Frame cross-connection	14	AT&T—Long Lines Dept. New York City	40
Comptroller's	Service order re-entry clerk	15	Pacific T&T Los Angeles	30
	Service order transcription clerk	16	Southern Bell Atlanta	20
	Keypuncher	17	Northwestern Bell Minnesota	13
Engineering	Equipment engineer	18	Michigan Bell Detroit	30
Traffic	Toll and information	19	Chesapeake & Potomac Virginia	*

Summary
19 trials
10 companies
9 jobs

*More than 2,000, but this trial differs in that it was open to any supervisors in the state. Therefore, no formal control is available. Judgments will be based on past performance of this group.

- Of all ages from 18 to 65.
- Of various educational levels.

This series of trials aims to answer the two-part question: (1) "Can a sample of Bell System jobs be loaded more heavily with responsibility and the other motivators following Herzberg's suggestion?" and (2) "Will there be large, measurable gains in deep job satisfaction?" The intent is to find a basis for making a global judgment—that is, a general judgment for the jobs and people involved in the studies. This intent will preclude such statements as, "*Yes* for this job or this department, but *no* for that job or that department." Valid results for a whole job or a whole department would call for very large samples in each case, perhaps as large as the total Bell System sample in this series of studies.

The conclusions, then, should be attached to Bell System people in general. They will be presented as *beliefs*, not proof positive, which are based on more evidence than we have ever had before.

No science ever proves anything finally. All it can do at any given time is state its propositions and cite the evidence in support. Later on, other scientists can correct the record. What is predicted in these studies is that deep satisfaction for more employees will result from a systematic effort to load jobs with the motivators named by Herzberg.

THE KINDS OF EVIDENCE

Before the start of this series of studies, four kinds of measurements of evidence were specified that should be systematically logged by the project directors. There was to be no fishing with a single pole. If changes occurred, this fishing *net* would bring them in. Changes, good or bad, were to be observed in:

Class 1	Technical measures of employee performance (numerous indexes, ratios, rates, and costs).
Class 2	Employee attitude (turnover, grievances, questionnaires).

| Class 3 | Customer attitude (Service Attitude Measurement or SAM complaints). |
| Class 4 | Managerial attitude (desire to drop project, to involve more employees, or to go from project to regular program). |

Turnover in Class 2, especially for young employees, those who can change jobs freely, is a good measure of job satisfaction whenever the economy of the nation is in good shape. This rate is used whenever possible, because unemployment in the United States during the years 1966 and 1967, when these studies were in progress, was generally quite low—between 3.5 and 3.9 percent nationally (4 percent is considered normal). In many of the test cities, unemployment was well below 4 percent and was actually below 2 percent in some of them. For older workers and those not free to "job hop" for whatever reason, the other classes or kinds of evidence are more relevant.

A special note about Class 4. Judgments are based on the quantitative indicators when possible, but Class 4, managerial attitude, is certainly used also. If the managers in the project groups do not like the approach used in the projects, if they do not want to expand the project voluntarily to cover other groups of their employees, *the final judgment has been made so far as the study is concerned.* In the 10 to 12 months of these projects, the managers soaked up far more than the formal evidence accumulated by the project director: They picked up the feelings of their subordinates, the unions, and other departments. Their synthesis, their final judgment, is crucial. If *they* won't have the project as a program, a regular way of operating for all their employees, it is doubtful that it can be legislated.

Long Lines Plant Trial

Let us make this all concrete by showing, in outline, one of the most revealing and educational trials in the new series (Trial 14). One of the groups of framemen in a certain building was plagued with the following problems:

1. Low productivity.
2. High frame errors.
3. Due dates missed.
4. Circuits that did not meet quality standards.
5. High overtime.
6. Grievances.

Within a huge central office, these men cross-connect wires of a long-distance switching point for telephone messages and many other kinds of communications.

Precise details as to what was going wrong prior to the trial can be found in the complete report in Appendix B. In a nutshell, the three-man teams, whose job is to connect wires to complete new communication circuits for customers, were limiting their output to an arbitrary number which was well below what could actually be done. As a result, customers were not getting their circuits on time unless overtime pay was forthcoming. In addition, too many circuits were failing to meet quality standards for the transmission of messages and others were connected with errors in them. The men were no happier than management was: They spoke of themselves as "frame apes," said the job required little ability, and entered many formal grievances through their union—about one per week. Help was requested by a boss who had read the report of the original study in Treasury.

The mental struggle in the workshop sessions to put more challenge into the work was enormous. Finally, at the end of a day's workshop, two second-level management men in the proposed project decided that the trouble was in the team setup. The 40 framemen involved were usually divided into teams of three. One worked at one end, soldering to a frame. The second ran the wire to a third man, who soldered the other end to a frame elsewhere in the huge building.

No team really had a full assignment—a full piece of work, a module. The men frequently did not know that their circuit work was inadequate because the circuit test group, another group of craftsmen, might not get to the new circuit until a later shift. And the cross-connection men never knew *whose* circuit they were working on, because still other craftsmen took the original service order and translated it into frame work to be done. The cross-connection men had no sense of "customer."

The two second-level supervisors came through with the first significant suggestion of a way to increase responsibility. They suggested combining the frame cross-connection group with the test group, dropping a cross-connection man, and adding a test man so that each three-man team has a test man on it from the start. That is Step 1 in Exhibit 8, an exhibit prepared by the supervisors themselves. Note that the supervisors plan eventually to collapse all five jobs so that *every* team has in it all five capabilities. At the start, each item represented a different job held by different men, all top-of-the-pay-scale craftsmen. Pay difference was not a problem. The cross-connections job was the one in trouble. The supervisors believed, initially, that the whole plan for enlarging this module or slice of work might take three to five years to execute. However, by the end of the trial they were predicting only two or three years because they found the men so eager to move ahead.

Exhibit 8

THE LONG LINES PLANT JOB—EXAMPLE OF ENRICHMENT
THROUGH CHANGING THE MODULE OF WORK

Private line service order
Loop testing   } Step 3
Circuit order write-up   } Step 4
Circuit testing   } Step 1   } Step 2
Cross-connections

In all the trials, one lesson learned was to work toward the end achieved here—to change or increase responsibility so that an employee could begin to feel a personal relationship with his work. Every job has its responsibilities or it would not exist; and these should be increased, for it is in responsibility that increased job satisfaction resides.

It is always possible to give recognition. But can *increased* responsibility and recognition for achievement be built directly into the work itself? By "recognition" individual feedback geared to individual performance is meant—not office indexes or other measures of how well a group of employees is performing, for even at best these are really measures of how well the supervisor is doing.

By adding a test man, the newly formed team knows immediately after completing a circuit whether it is a complete circuit, whether it meets quality standards, and—by trying to contact the customer directly upon completion of the circuit—whether a frame error has been made. This is well within the definition of individual feedback even though three men are involved, for if there is an error the team will know virtually every time what went wrong. No office index for all 40 men will do this job well, although it will tell the supervisor —or the director of the project—whether the office as a whole is going along all right.

If it can be said that an art has been developed, it centers on the process of finding meaningful new items of responsibility. In the Long Line Plant trial, the goal might simply be summarized as follows:

Work to be done	Customer requires a new circuit.
Before the trial	One team writes up order; a second team makes the connection; a third team tests the circuit; manager receives unit index on errors.
End of trial	One team does all work from write-up to turning over working circuit to customer.

We've learned that, with a little help, lists of greater responsibilities, ways of giving improved feedback, and opportunities to learn something new can be made by the supervisors. For example, a district Traffic man, his chief operator, and her group chiefs can build a starting list of 50 to 100 items by the end of a two-day workshop. In no trial in any department have fewer than 25 items been put forth. The final lists of items to be implemented in the trials to be reported generally contain 10 to 20.

At one stage in the workshop the familiar "creative thinking" or "wild thinking" approach was used in this way: The leader announced that a "green light" was on, figuratively. While it was on, he wanted the group to toss out ideas for increasing responsibility (and the other motivators listed in the preceding chapter) as fast as he could write them on easel sheets. He warned them that no one was to throw a "red light," thus stopping the flow of ideas, upon pain of some nameless, horrible fate. Typical red lights would be: "That will never work"; "We tried that before"; and just plain signs of alarm and dismay. Here is the final list of greenlight items for the Long Lines Plant trial.

1. Perform both equipment and transmission work.
2. Perform overall circuit testing.
3. Direct cross-connection job.
4. Represent groups at meetings.
5. Act as team leader.
6. Appoint team leader replacement.
7. Determine work priority.
8. Negotiate temporary force changes.
9. Make first-level and second-level management contacts.
10. Negotiate with customers for circuit releases.
11. Issue memos.
12. Conduct orientation of new employees and tours of visitors.

These are the survivors of an original list many times longer. Items 1 and 2 were extremely important. Note Items 9 and 10 also. If necessary, a craftsman now talks directly to first- and second-level management people in other central offices or in his own building when a circuit is involved. He does not have to talk to his boss, who would then telephone the other boss. And he talks directly to customers. (A customer can be another Bell System person as well as an outsider.)

It is not known exactly which ideas are the key ones. Perhaps they have the effect of a shotgun blast; it is the whole charge that brings the beast down.

The group is currently performing virtually all its work on schedule, as Exhibit 9 indicates. At the start of the trial when the group consisted of 40 men, their on-time performance was frequently at the 50 percent level. The number of men required increased to

Exhibit 9

Percent Circuit Order Items Completed on Schedule

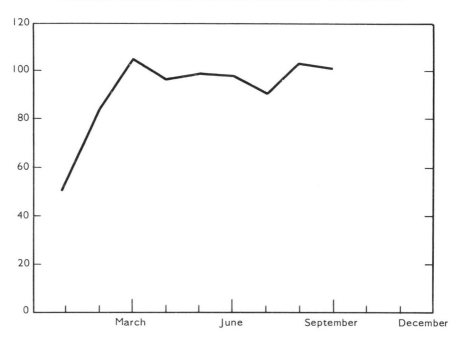

Exhibit 10

Overtime Hours

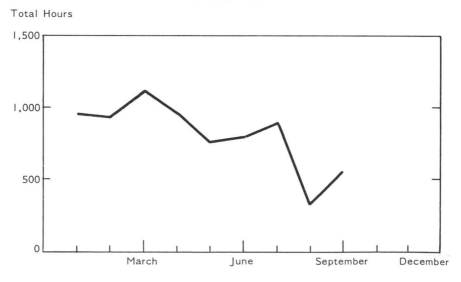

42 soon after the trial started, and then it dropped to 35, where it stood at the end of the trial.

Remember, also, that overtime had been a problem. Note in Exhibit 10 that overtime hours have decreased about 50 percent since the work-itself study began. This is a particularly significant drop because, although there are fewer men, they are getting the work done without going into an offsetting overtime situation.

As Exhibit 11 indicates, the old arbitrary restriction by the men on their output simply disappeared. Output had been limited to a certain number of jumpers or parts of circuits, a fact known to men and management but not discussed. Now the men complete the circuits and don't seem to worry about the number of jumpers

Exhibit 11

NUMBER CIRCUIT ORDER
ITEMS COMPLETED

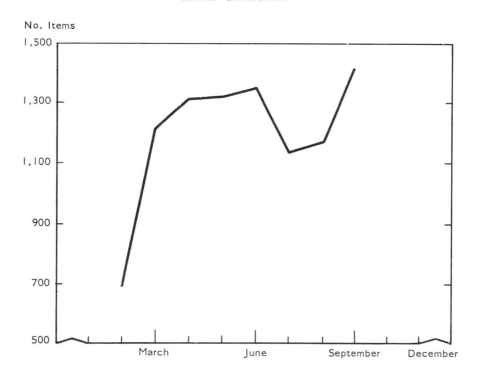

Exhibit 12

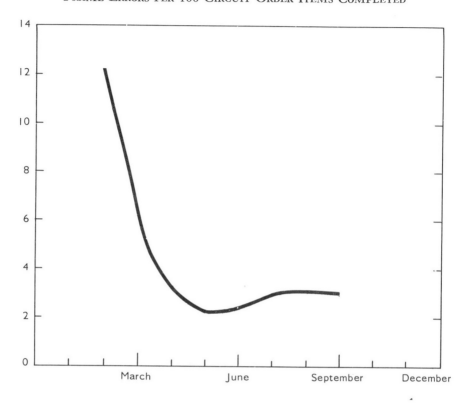

FRAME ERRORS PER 100 CIRCUIT ORDER ITEMS COMPLETED

involved. The improvement shown in Exhibit 11 is great, with some setback in July and August because of vacations. Since this is a new measure, there are no control data available. These good results are due solely to the day tour since the night tour still has not gone onto this plan; it still limits its "jumpers completed," which tends to hold back the total effort. Therefore, only part of the total force and Step 1 of Exhibit 8 have produced the excellent results of this trial.

Frame errors, it will be recalled, had previously been a most serious problem. Now look at them (Exhibit 12)! Now the men talk about "my circuit" and "my customer." They establish work priorities themselves and start the day immediately; no queuing up and waiting for the supervisor to give them work. And, when leaving a tour, they hand work directly to those coming in, which pleases supervisors too. Not only do the men enjoy checking circuits to see if they will meet test standards the first time; they are also asking when they will get certain new training.

While a number of other valuable gains can be noted in Appendix B, let us end here with this quotation from that report. It's hard to beat. "Perhaps one of the most meaningful observations is the fact that no formal union grievances were received from this group during the entire period of the study. Prior to the beginning of the project, grievances averaged about one each week." As this trial progressed, a much more informal relationship developed between men and bosses. Items that might have been grievances previously do not become so now. But we must not forget the priority of events; first the basic job improved, then the better relations developed.

Why pick this framemen trial for detailed presentation? It was chosen because it clearly illustrates the following major points for the manager who wants to improve the work itself.

1. Results of excessive fragmentation of work.
2. Steps to reconstitute it.
3. Ways to handle individual differences.
4. Need for elastic job boundaries.
5. Importance of a meaningful slice of work for good performance and job satisfaction.

Item 3, on handling individual differences, deserves a brief elaboration. By the end of the trial (eight months), only 14 of the 35 men had taken on half or more of the new responsibilities cited in the final greenlight list. Some men are more capable, more eager to learn and to go forward than others, and this approach, with its elastic job boundaries (Item 4), permits flexibility in dealing with people. The new job freedoms and job responsibilities are not treated as something in short supply, like money. Any man can have any responsibility he can handle; it's up to him and his boss. By the time all five jobs are collapsed (see Exhibit 8), three years may have gone by for any one man. The job should be truly rich and responsible by then. If it is that, then the safest prediction is further improvements in job performance (Item 5). Meaningful work is what intelligent people seek; it leads to good performance, self-satisfying performance. It seems evident from the study that good performance leads to job satisfaction, not the other way around.

Another point might be added to the list. There is a natural tendency to fragment or fractionalize a job *still further* when conflict arises between men and management over a piece of work. The management head who first asked that this job situation be studied remarked, when he saw the proposal for recombining jobs, that *he* might have fragmented the troublesome job still more. If these men did not want to do the cross-connecting work, he might have gotten some tall unemployed people for some shelves and short unemployed people for others or in some other way have specialized the job still further. "Try to find grateful people," he said.

A major inference from this study that is supported by other studies in the series is this: When jobs get into trouble, beware of further fragmentation. Fragmentation probably comes about normally. As the telephone switching machine is improved and as other tools and instruments in the total business take over part of the human effort, mere pieces of jobs may be left.

Service Representative Trials

Consider the results of all eight service representative trials as a whole. The service representative is the employee a customer reaches to order a new telephone, remove or relocate an existing one, question a bill or an item on the bill, get a new directory to replace one that has been destroyed, and so on. The "rep's" job is a complex one, and as new telephone services proliferate the job will probably become more complex. Training requires approximately eight weeks—a longer period in urban areas, where there are complex business accounts, than in small towns. When a rep is lost through preventable turnover, some manager may say, "Well, there goes $2,500!"

Turnover because of resignation or dismissal among all reps has been trending upward from about 20 percent in 1962 to nearly 30 percent in 1967, as shown earlier in Exhibit 1. Keen interest at headquarters in improving this job led to making this the biggest single effort in the series of studies. Eight complete telephone districts in four associated companies were on the achieving side, matched as well as possible with eight on the control side—more than 800 repre-sentatives, about 3 percent of the Bell System total. See what has been accomplished in these urban districts, which is where turn-over hits hardest.

Turnover.[1] In seven out of the eight service representative trials, there was a decrease in the percentage of resignations and dismissals for the achieving groups as compared to the control groups. In an average of straight percentages, the achieving groups in all eight trials netted 20 percent less turnover than the control groups. Be-cause of the wide range of group sizes (19 to 83), it is perhaps more meaningful to examine the turnover data in terms of actual numbers of losses. (See Exhibit 13.)

In actual numbers, the achieving population as a whole lost 57 fewer service representatives than the control groups, whereas in the comparable period a year earlier it had lost 33 more. A formal test of statistical significance (chi-square) indicated that the probability of such a change resulting solely from mere random variation is less than one in a hundred.

As shown in the last line of Exhibit 13, while turnover got worse by 9.3 percent in the control groups, it improved 13.1 percent in the achieving groups. Therefore, the actual net turnover gain in absolute terms is 22.4 percent. With regard to their respective start-ing points, however, the relative turnover in the control groups *increased* by 33 percent while that in the achieving groups as a whole decreased by 34 percent. This far exceeded our wildest hopes and may never be achieved again with such large numbers of em-ployees.

How much was saved on training costs alone? The best estimate of what *would have* happened in the achieving group had there been no trial is what actually *did* happen in the control groups. Note first that the two groups were almost exactly the same size at the start of the trial: 398 as compared to 396. While the control group lost 42 more reps in this period than in a comparable six-month period the year before, the achieving group saved 48 reps. It can safely be assumed that, at $2,500 per person, these 90 reps would have cost not less than $225,000 to train.

The job market is wide open for competent, well-trained young

[1]The turnover and service sections of this chapter are from a specially prepared analysis and report by Harold Dunkelman.

Exhibit 13

RESIGNATIONS AND DISMISSALS—ACTUAL NUMBERS
SERVICE REPRESENTATIVES

| Trial Locations | Achieving Group | | | Control Groups | | | Net Diff. |
	(1) Before	(2) After[1]	(3) Diff.[2]	(4) Before	(5) After	(6) Diff.	Cols. (3) minus (6)
Toronto	27	14	−13	35	25	−10	− 3
Montreal	22	16	− 6	12	24	+12	−18
Chicago—City	2	8	+ 6	8	20	+12	− 6
Suburban Office 1	2	6	+ 4	5	2	− 3	+ 7
Suburban Office 2	11	7	− 4	2	13	+11	−15
Rhode Island	31	27	− 4	24	24	0	− 4
Northern Massachusetts	26	11	−15	26	50	+24	−39
Maryland	34	18	−16	10	6	− 4	−12
Total losses	155	107	−48	122	164	+42	−90
No. service representatives on roll	398	414		396	409		
Percentage of resignations and dismissals	38.9	25.8	−13.1	30.8	40.1	+ 9.3	−22.4

[1] "After" period refers to the last six months of the trials; "before" period is the comparable time span one year earlier.
[2] A minus sign indicates losses (turnover) decreased; a plus sign, that turnover worsened.

service representatives in areas such as airlines, department stores, utilities, and banks. The difference in turnover in this instance is therefore a sensitive indicator of a changed attitude toward work. Turnover is still higher than desired in the achieving groups. At the end of the trial, it was at 25.8 percent owing to resignations and dismissals. However, the significant fact is that the tide of turnover was at last reversed.

Service. It is important to know that this decreased turnover has not been achieved at the expense of customer service. Data for many technical indicators of this were collected in the eight locations, in both achieving and control. Some of the many indicators were:

- Composite customer service index.
- Errors in service.
- Irregularities.
- Slow service.
- Customer service attitude measurement (SAM).

When the data were analyzed in the field and then reanalyzed at headquarters of AT&T, this conservative statement was agreed upon: "The appreciable gains in turnover are certainly not at the expense of providing good service." In fact, the majority view is that technical indexes will improve noticeably over the long run as the force of reps stabilizes and becomes more experienced.

Changes in the job. What was changed in the job of the service representatives to bring about this substantial improvement in the turnover rate? Items such as the six that follow are merely a sample; all of them are aimed at giving a bright young person full responsibility for dealing with a customer.

1. Service representative (SR) determines credit ratings of a customer without business office supervisor's (BOS) approval.
2. SR determines amount of deposit and whether one is required from a customer without BOS approval.
3. SR may deny service for nonpayment without BOS or manager's approval.
4. SR signs adjustment vouchers and submits to accounting without BOS approval. (Example: giving a customer $1.85 credit for a call made by someone else.)
5. Accounting returns all vouchers in error directly to originating SR.

6. Where used, customers' service attitude measurement questionnaires are returned to SR directly.

In a trial situation, responsibilities such as these six are pushed on a rep as fast as possible. She is trained; she is encouraged to try to do these things herself; she is given *direct* feedback when possible (not through a supervisor). And, if she cannot learn to do it or if she does not like a responsible job, we say, "Find some other job for her in the telephone company that matches her capabilities." This is the stance on all these projects with both male and female employees.

The first four items illustrate some new responsibilities for the service representative, while the last two items illustrate direct feedback. In no one trial would all six of these examples be found. But in every trial there would be a list this long or longer. Final lists in general ran to about 30 items.

The simple truth is that it's not the six or the sixteen formal items alone. Rather, the question is this: Can the supervisor join in this job improvement effort every day by giving a valued employee the last word in making a decision about some new matter that has come up? Or will the supervisor say, "This is what I think you should do; please do it and tell me how it comes out"?

Finally, it should be noted that in this instance there was no need to combine the service representative's job with that of the teller (who handles customer payments), the service order typist, or anyone else.

On the other hand, in not one instance did the supervisors suggest that the job of the service representative be improved by fragmenting it further. In fact, in several instances they blocked a tendency to set up a few new specialized service representative desks, such as a final payments desk, to which a rep would send her bills when the likelihood of collection was nearing zero. The supervisors decided to abandon this approach on the grounds that each rep must be held responsible for the collection of her own final payments. The consensus is that the module is good as it is and that improvement can be made within it.

After an opportunity for reflection at the end of the trials, the coordinator of all eight Commercial Department projects, W. L. Dytrt, sketched out Exhibit 14. This exhibit shows a shift away

Exhibit 14

THE SERVICE REPRESENTATIVE'S RESPONSIBILITY FOR COLLECTION

	Here's Where We Are Today	*Here's What Some Districts Are Doing*	
Manager	Approves denial of service. Decides final disposition of any account item.	Is responsible for developing supervisor.	
Business Office Supervisor	Approves size of customer deposits and credit classifications. Prepares treatment schedules for delinquent accounts. Approves extensions of credit. Audits treatment files.	Is responsible for coaching and developing service representative to level of competency to handle assignments.	
Service Representative	Carries out decisions of others.	Earns responsibility for the work itself.	
		Deposits and credit classifications.	Makes final account disposition.
		Treatment schedules.	Performance feedback.
		Extensions of credit.	Joint treatment file review with supervisor.
		Denials.	Posts own write-off record. Maintains own collection report.

from carrying out someone else's decisions and toward active participation in making those decisions. This is the heart of responsibility as applied to the collection of bills. Similar diagrams could be drawn for other parts of this job.

Even though this is the most thoroughly explored job, there is strong agreement with the managers of the various commercial departments involved that it would be profitable to go farther; they have strongly backed an extended effort. It was indicated earlier that managerial attitude would be examined as one of four kinds of evidence. Realistically, however, it is the last word. Let us leave the matter at this point and consider the results from other departmental trials, then return to managerial decisions about the projects at the end of this chapter.

COMPTROLLER'S TRIALS

Three Comptroller's trials, shown in Exhibit 15, range from an older job, keypunch operator, to one associated with a most advanced computer, that of the service order re-entry clerk. In all three, results have been so good that Comptroller employees at AT&T headquarters are enthusiastic, and with good reason. For example, if the volume of work could have been held constant, the number of employees in each of the three groups would have dropped relative to control groups. In fact, this actually did happen in Los Angeles. In the other trials, rising volumes of work offset the fact that fewer people were needed for the existing work.

What was learned from these trials is that removing employees from their jobs by fiat does not achieve these results. Conceivably, a percentage cut might make the jobs of those who remain even worse. The basic approach is to load people with responsibility—to build in direct, personal feedback. Then, as a result of fallout, you find you don't need so many checkers, verifiers, work assigners, and "pushers" of various kinds. Beginning with the Treasury trial, this unanticipated and unplanned consequence has repeatedly emerged. The reality of this phenomenon can hardly be challenged now.

Take the Keypunch trial, for example. The sizable gains came after each girl got her own kinds of cards to punch (say, payroll for a department). As she developed, she had the right to question

Exhibit 15

COMPTROLLER'S TRIALS

Job	Location	Gain Noted	Final Rating*
Keypunch operator	Minneapolis	Quality Production Turnover drop Absence drop Employee attitude (questionnaire)	Quite successful
Service order transcription clerk	Atlanta	Productivity Quality Turnover drop	Modestly successful
Service order re-entry clerk	Los Angeles	Productivity Employee attitude (questionnaire) Quality	Quite successful

* A consensus of the views of the project director, the managers involved in the trial, and the responsible departmental staff persons in the associated company and at AT&T, New York.

the department about the input, she helped set her own deadline dates, and she was responsible for scheduling and arranging her work to meet the various deadlines. She could set the verification rate herself based upon a feedback of the accuracy of her punching. She became known as the expert on certain assignments. Quite clearly, the usual approach was avoided wherein one employee served as assignment clerk and distributed work as it came along. So too were a number of unnecessary supervisory reviews. Thus fewer employees eventually were needed. A partial list of greenlight items for the trial follows:

1. Each clerk will be assigned a recognizable module of work that she will be responsible for punching each day or week; that is, payrolls for a certain department, labor for particular groups, and so on.

2. Each clerk will investigate and when possible correct any input errors; that is, those she recognizes prior to keypunching. Formerly, these were routed to her supervisor for reference to an appropriate group.
3. Clerks will maintain their own quality and quantity records. In the past, these were maintained by an assignment clerk or supervisor.
4. Each clerk will be given direct feedback on output errors. Clerks will be notified of any errors in keypunching and will make necessary corrections. Previously this was done by an assignment clerk or a verifier.
5. A sample key verification is based on record of accuracy; clerks will have a sample of their work verified, rather than 100 percent of their work.
6. Each clerk will be given definite assignments and due dates. With these in mind, clerks will schedule their own work to meet the job requirements.

Detailed supporting charts and tables for all trials are omitted to save space. However, the keypunch and service order re-entry clerk results are as striking as those in the framemen's trial or the original Treasury trial.

The service order re-entry clerk's job is of great interest because it involves new jobs connected with a big new computer that serves more than a million accounts. (It is quite possible, we have learned, to set up a job poorly right from the start.) The women involved were senior clerks; their average age was 35. As was true in the framemen's trial, turnover was nil, but productivity was poor. The final report remarks, "There did not appear to be any evidence that the employees identified themselves with anything other than an eight-hour task to perform." Therefore, several of the green-light items tried to give a clerk "something of her own"—a few large customer accounts as well as some regular small ones.

Under the heading "Subjective Results" the final report for this project reads:

> One of the clerks who handles a very large customer account, which was converting to a new and difficult telephone system, attended an interdepartmental meeting to plan the cutover.

She was so pleased to go and talk about *her* account that her husband bought her a new dress for the meeting. Throughout the cutover, she was genuinely concerned over the eventual results. This is an interested, motivated employee. She has the responsibility and thrives on it.

Supervisors are now back in the business of management and are more available to their people than ever before. Problems are now being worked out as much as possible by the clerks, and they only ask for help when they are truly unable to find a remedy. With that much more time available, the first-line supervisors are able to develop and analyze potential among their people.

In this instance, the number of senior clerks needed to perform the same workload dropped from 23 to 15. Their report says, "The decrease in workforce was caused by reduction in verification, consolidation of jobs, and elimination of some 'fat' which existed." A top specialist in the Comptroller's Department remarked when he saw these data, "Whenever we are confronted with bad results, we tend to set up a new line of verifiers. And when we do that, I suppose we have not sacrificed our amateur standing as managers."

The concluding paragraph of their report is especially noteworthy because no department in the Bell System is now faced with a period of greater change than is the Comptroller's as it finds new ways to manage the paper flood.

In order to take advantage of the theme of the work motivation theory, we must apply the basics to the jobs that are now in existence. With the rapid changes and large-scale redesign of accounting operations in the next five to ten years, the need for employees who will work with us, instead of for us, is more than ever apparent. Let's start by doing things *for* people instead of *to* them.

Traffic Trials

The consensus of ratings on the three Traffic trials is "modestly successful" (see Exhibit 16). "Traffic" is the Bell System's name for the very large department which operates the switchboards. Saginaw's turnover rate dropped six percentage points from 29 percent, while the company's increased by two points.[2] These are the rates for operators with six months or more of service—the only operators given any of their 13 greenlight items. They divided their list into four fairly simple items and nine more complicated items.

Exhibit 16

TRAFFIC TRIALS

Job	Location	Gain Noted	Final Rating[1]
1. Toll operator	Saginaw, Michigan	Turnover drop Management reaction	Modestly successful
2. Overseas toll	Long Lines, New York City	Turnover drop Employee attitude (questionnaire) Technical results (various)	Modestly successful
3. Toll and information	Virginia, statewide[2]	Employee attitude Management reaction	Modestly successful

[1] Consensus of the views of project director, managers involved in the trial, and the responsible departmental staff persons in the associated company and at AT&T, New York.
[2] No control available.

The management reaction was measured in this way. The supervisors in the achieving groups were told at the end of the trial that the trial was now over and they were free to return to their former practices—that is, to simply drop the greenlight items. If the supervisors refused (which was the case in almost all trials in all departments) and if instead the approach was spread as a *program* within

[2]In the six months after the formal trial ended, Saginaw dropped another two points while the company increased by another point.

the department, then management reaction is noted in the "Gain Noted" column. (Management reaction could have been used much more freely than it has been.)

In Long Lines, the achieving group of overseas operators improved in 7 out of 11 technical measurements, while a control group of similar operators improved in only 2 out of 11. Again the turnover rate dropped for the achievers, whereas it worsened in the control group. The list of greenlight items totals 35 and is divided into 4 levels of increasing responsibility. Typical items from these trials include the following:

1. Use my own words, rather than standard phrases, in speaking with customers and other operators.
2. Take part in inducting and coaching new employees.
3. Select one hour's work, the performance of which I will discuss with my group chief operator.
4. Determine myself when to suggest that a customer might want to make his own subsequent attempt.
5. Handle all contacts with the plant involving equipment failure and circuit conditions.
6. Adjust charges myself and notify the customer.

Permeating these large, older organizations with new ideas is hard, but it can be done. However, the study design that was employed elsewhere almost caused the loss of the Traffic trials. Attempts to control the "Hawthorne effect," a phenomenon familiar to social scientists, were at the heart of the difficulty.

For many years, at least since certain famous Harvard University studies were made in the Hawthorne Plant of the Bell System's Western Electric Company, social scientists have been aware that studies which involve people are subject to a peculiar hazard: When they know they are being studied, people do not react in the way they would if they did not know a study was in progress. TV viewers of "Candid Camera" have seen this phenomenon repeatedly. The moment the person hears, "You're on Candid Camera!" he abandons his natural behavior. In the entertainment world, this is called "kleig light effect." Chemicals are indifferent to the chemist but people seldom are to the social scientist. They are "fer" him or "agin" him and his ideas. Whether it is conscious or subconscious, the phenomenon must be reckoned with.

The decision for all 19 studies was therefore *not* to tell the clerks, the operators, the craftsmen, and others who held the jobs that were being changed. This rule was never violated so far as project directors could ascertain. Thus only changes in the *work itself* would be causing the hoped-for better results.

This is not to say that employees were unaware that things were being done differently. But changes are always being made in the way work is to be done; merely changing work or work assignments of a Monday morning isn't news; it's the supervisor's normal routine. But the supervisors did not say, "This is a step in a project aimed at . . ."

The desire to avoid the Hawthorne effect also led to the decision not to tell *even the first-level supervisor* why the job changes were coming down from managers at the second level and higher (those who had created the greenlight list). The changes were always suggested as routine efforts to achieve better job performance, not as a test of a theory of motivation.

In the case of Traffic, however (at least in Long Lines and in Virginia), it was necessary to change the strategy and include the first level supervisor (group chief operator). It appears now that where employee groups are very large or where they have complicated work schedules causing relatively fleeting and impersonal contacts between supervisor and employee, the lowest level of supervision must fully understand the new project, or the old habits will not permit implementation of the new ideas.

Therefore, the group chiefs were also given the chance to hear the story behind this work and to build their own greenlight lists— items for change in operator performance. Actually, there is yet another sublevel or half-level of supervision between the group chief and the operators known variously as service assistants or service supervisors. In no case were they informed or included in the workshop sessions. The group chief is, formally, the first level of management in Traffic. To control the Hawthorne effect in these 19 studies, neither operators nor their service assistants were involved.

The near loss of the Traffic trials leads to the strong recommendation that first-line managers be included in all programs, as distinguished from projects. At the program stage, gains from maintenance items, the Hawthorne effect, or any other source will be welcome, for the problem of job satisfaction is deeply rooted. At the end of these trials, it is still the belief that improving the work itself will be the fundamental and most radical change. The Hawthorne effect, change in maintenance items, and so on will probably have only short-range motivational effects.

Since there was no suitable control group in the Virginia Traffic trial (all district managers—the third level of management— for the whole state were given the option of being in it), that trial was used primarily to learn what happens when you try to reach several hundred management people. This was not a "project" but rather a "program"—an ongoing, day-to-day effort in which everyone was free to talk and exchange ideas. Of the many things that emerged, two salient points were these:

1. Quite clearly, some *supervisors* want to be last in line; a year later a small number have not yet asked to be included.
2. Some 10 or 15 percent of the *employees* actually do not want any more responsibility. For example, 2 operators in a group of 23 returned the loose-leaf binders in which they had been asked to keep and analyze Xerox copies of their defective billing tickets and watch the trend from month to month, show the traffic load they carried, and analyze the quality of their service. Such analysis, they said, had traditionally been done by management and they felt it was management's job, not theirs. Happily, 85 percent or more do not feel that way; perhaps emphasis should be placed on *their* interest in being responsible for their own results, for this attitude is certainly typical.

PLANT TRIALS

In addition to the trial at the Long Lines Plant, there were two other plant trials. (See Exhibit 17.) One of these ended in no gain and no loss; the trial was finally postponed because of certain local conditions. But even in this case the final report speaks favorably of the main improving idea, which was to give each installer his own city blocks and as much telephone work of various kinds as he could possibly handle. The men like the idea. One installer wrote a glowing (and accurate) report of what he had accomplished in his own area; this is used in Chapter 7 to illustrate the importance and the appeal of having one's own place, territory, or area of responsibility.

Exhibit 17

PLANT TRIALS

Job	Location	Gain Noted	Final Rating*
Frame cross-connection	Long Lines, New York City	Productivity Grievance drop Quality Employee attitude	Quite successful
Station installation	Chicago	Management reaction Customer satisfaction (SAM)	Modestly successful
Station installation	(Large Urban)	?	Not successful

*Consensus of the views of project director, managers involved in the trial, and the responsible departmental staff persons in the associated company and at AT&T, New York.

Exhibit 18

ENGINEERING TRIAL

Job	Location	Gains Noted	Final Rating*
Step-by-step equipment engineer	Michigan	Employee attitude Management reaction	Modestly successful

*Consensus of the views of project director, managers involved in the trial, and the responsible departmental staff persons in the associated company and at AT&T, New York.

The three Plant trials, then, range from "outstanding" to "zero." The conclusion to be drawn from this is not that the Plant Department is different, but simply that this approach to improving jobs does not automatically bring success. Chapters 5 and 6 contain plausible insights regarding the reasons *why* some projects go well while others do not. These insights lack any departmental identification, for this would not advance understanding or the general purpose of the work-itself trials.

Engineering Trial

The trial among step-by-step (step-by-step is a type of central office equipment) equipment engineers, shown in Exhibit 18, is hard to measure because there are no readily available indexes in the Engineering Department. Nevertheless, the chief engineer and his staff wanted to try out the idea of improving jobs for these well-paid, intelligent men, and so did the top engineers at AT&T in New York, who advised on personnel matters in their department. The key change was to give each engineer a modular assignment in order to establish accountability. For example, in the step-by-step trial group, each engineer was given a definite area (they call it real estate) with specific offices. A map of the state was made and the number of central offices was balanced out by expected workload. Then each engineer was asked how he felt about taking his own designated area. He would have full responsibility in the office in his area.

All in the group agreed to this. One engineer said, "I've been here 15 years and this is the first time I've felt that I had a job of my own." One sizable geographic area went to a young engineer with only 18 months' service in his company. At the end of the trial period, his boss told him that he was doing a splendid job. The young man said, "Frankly, I never expected to be given such a responsible job." It is now known that the other departments and the chief suppliers (Plant, Traffic, and the Western Electric Company) all like the fact that they have *one* engineer to call when they have questions or need help and that they can call this engineer directly.

It is important to avoid oversimplifying engineering problems.

In other instances, this geographic approach might have its drawbacks. But it is not the distribution of territory, it's the giving of responsibility that is important. If there is some other way to help a man establish a personal relationship with his work, do it! In this case mere territorial assignments helped. This change was only one of 27 related changes, but the majority keyed in on this geographic (or modular) change. In a real sense, it came first.

After Michigan Engineering had reviewed its first effort, it actually went ahead in a companywide program because the reaction of both engineers and management was favorable. This reaction is the basis for saying the trial is at least modestly successful. It is regrettable that "harder" data are not available.

A Reaction and a Decision

In general, those who participated in the original Treasury Department project and those who have since entered the program have valued the concepts highly. So far as is known, virtually no one in the program says, "It won't work." As the educational effort described in Appendix A continues from month to month and as results are achieved similar to those summarized in Chapter 2, the number of doubters from outside the program grows smaller.

Both during each new trial and at its conclusion, there was an attempt to make either a formal or an informal appraisal of the reactions of the three lower management levels, those closely involved in implementing the ideas with employees in the target jobs. Sometimes tape recordings were made to provide a present and future basis for analysis.

One broadly based generalization can be stated: The levels of supervision closest to the projects strongly support the work-itself concepts. These supervisors were usually asked this general question: "When the trial period has ended, what do you plan to do?" Often the question would actually provoke alarm. "You don't mean we're going to have to go back to our old way, do you?" "I'll never go back to the old way of running things as long as I'm a boss."

Even more substantial proof of the viability of the notions and procedures is that the bosses often applied these ideas to related jobs on their own initiative. In every Traffic trial, for example, some group chief operators have greenlighted the job of the service assistant. This was not officially encouraged, but no suggestion was made that it be stopped either. If the idea of extending the project to related jobs came up for open discussion, the usual suggestion was, "Wait till the end of the project. It won't be long."

At middle- and top-management levels, the very act of presenting final results has precipitated a desire to spread the concepts—to turn projects into programs—virtually without exception. Even within the associated company (where the only "zero-result" trial occurred), the other trial, in the Comptroller's organization, turned out very well. As a result, that company is going ahead, knowing full well that success is not automatically assured when a project or program starts.

How do managers feel, then? At lower levels where direct contact occurred and at upper levels where results were reviewed these projects have been very well received. Results are still being presented and courses of action are still being determined, making a meaningful inventory of proposed actions impossible. Clearly, however, the programs are endorsed by top management. The key elements in the approval are these:

1. A manpower utilization program is to continue, with job improvement as a key concept.
2. It will be no "crash" program; managers will not be pushed into going along; the program must be made attractive to them.
3. Work-itself concepts are to be inserted into every basic supervisory training program.
4. There must be the "right reason" for going ahead: to make sure that every employee has as self-fulfilling and responsible a job as possible.
5. The costs of the effort must be kept in mind. Evidence indicates costs will be self-liquidating because of improvement in motivation to work.

RESULTS OF THE TRIALS—A CONCLUSION

What conclusions can be drawn from all 19 trials? Certainly the original Treasury Department group of female correspondents was not typical of Bell System workers in general. But these girls were typical of modern young workers—they lack the economic fears of their parents and will quit rather than keep jobs they don't want. The persistent need in the job market for bright young people indicates, in fact, that their appraisal of the job situation is correct. They do not need to keep an unsatisfactory job.

The question of the sampling adequacy of the new series of studies must be stressed: It is *not* a good sample of the Bell System, even though more than 1,000 employees are on the experimental side with an equal number on the control, and even though all major departments are in the sample. Therefore, it was decided that no case would be made for the results unless the differences were large and unless operating managers considered them important differences.

The differences in the original Treasury trial *were* large. According to Treasury officials, the results elsewhere in Treasury since then are impressive. The results in the eight service representative trials are quite large; in fact, this is the best single sample. The accounting trials' results in the Comptroller's Department are visible and consistent. Those in Traffic, Plant, and Engineering Departments are not as large and impressive, relatively, but one would have to consider them modest gains.

There were no trials in which the achieving group came off *worse* than control, but there was one trial that should be clearly labeled "no difference."

Thus the conclusion that can be drawn from these trials is that the attempt to upgrade the work itself through job improvement procedures is well worth the time and effort of any manager who believes, after analyzing turnover data, that he has a motivational problem on his hands. Inroads were made on the turnover problem in many of these trials at a time when not many personnel people had any other advice to offer. To say "It's a symptom of the times in which we live" or "It's correlated with the economic cycle" is not to offer useful advice. Yet the problem can be attacked, not merely accepted.

For older employees, such as the senior clerks in the service order re-entry job or the Long Lines Plant men, turnover is not a sensitive indicator of trouble. The same procedures yielded good results, but other indicators picked up the change (productivity, quality of work, and so on). Since union officials do not oppose the idea of giving employees more freedom on their jobs, there was no conflict over the trials.

In early 1968, top management of the Bell System decided to let managers go ahead on a *program* basis (not merely as trial projects) when and where they want to. Within the year, newly trained leaders started 77 new programs, scheduled another 46 for early 1969, and planned more to follow these. This is, in a very real sense, the most substantial proof of the success of the projects to date.

4

A Critical Visit
to a Work-Itself Site

IN ONE COMMERCIAL DEPARTMENT OF AN ASSOCIATED COMPANY
that had not joined in the eight trials involving service representatives, the operating managers decided to take a hard look at the
results. A team of three middle management men was then dis-
patched to an associated company where one of the trials reported in
Chapter 3 had taken place.

Each man appraised results in the area of Commercial operations
which he knew best, and all three also assessed the current status.
The formal trial period had ended a year earlier. Had the effort—
once adjudged a success—disappeared without a trace? This was an
especially rigorous test because the coordinator who had been tend-
ing the project was assigned to new tasks after the project closed.

The district commercial manager (third level) who had been
responsible for the project welcomed the three managers and turned
them over to his unit managers (second level). Trial locations themselves are protected from such visits during the course of a trial.

The report which follows was written by Robert H. Janson,

one of the team members. It is a consensus of findings and was intended for exclusive use in their company. In contrast to the objective approach of Chapter 3, it will give some feeling for and understanding of the emotional reactions of those people directly involved in a project. It is based on intensive interviewing by the three experienced operating managers. They say frankly that their attitude was one of polite skepticism, but that they were open to persuasion. In this printed version, names and places have been changed to protect the trial district from unsolicited visits.

A CRITICAL APPRAISAL OF A
WORK-ITSELF PROJECT—BY ROBERT H. JANSON

In June 1968 three managers visited "A" district to study and evaluate the work-itself program that began in May 1966 and was completed the following spring. The purpose of the visit was to evaluate, from a line point of view, the results of the work-itself concept in relation to our own districts. We conducted our interviews with a random selection of employees in the district so as to avoid prepared presentations. We believed that this would help us objectively evaluate success or failure.

"A" district is primarily residential (approximately 80 percent residential accounts and 20 percent business accounts); it serves 210,000 customers and bills roughly $3 million per month. This large district, which is situated in the southern part of the city, is composed of three manager units, each divided into business and residence groups. It also has an order-processing unit with 20 employees and a manager. The district manager has been in the district approximately one year; the managers—all in their middle thirties—have been there somewhat longer and seem experienced.

INTERVIEWS

Max—manager. Max has been on the job for about one year and has implemented the work-itself program since his promotion. He has three supervisors reporting to him: One has thirteen years' experience; the two others have less than a year.

The work-itself concept is utilized throughout his unit. Max's responsibilities entail only developmental control; all other control items and details had been completely delegated to the supervisors and representatives.

Jane—supervisor. Max's newest supervisor, Jane, has been in her present capacity less than a year. Prior to her promotion, she had been a representative for the same period of time. In her section are six representatives, three with three years' experience, two with less than a year, and one with six months.

The smoothness of Jane's operation and her freedom from burdensome routines were indicated by the fact that her desk was devoid of the usual clutter of forms and her telephone never rang during the interview. When asked what was the exact nature of her job, Jane presented us with a work-itself manual and said her job was to develop and motivate her people. She had no control lists or performance sheets because the representatives in her section maintained their own personal records. She told us that she performed no supervisory checks except on new representatives and that, once she was assured of a worker's competence, the girl was assigned the responsibility of her own desk. Routine forms which previously required Jane's signature were now signed by the representatives themselves. In a normal eight-hour working day, Jane spends only an hour and a half on supervisory routines, devoting the remaining hours to developing her people.

Laura—representative. Laura has been a representative for three years and has been in the work-itself district one year. When she was asked her opinion of the two job environments, she proceeded to discuss a lengthy list of work items for which she was now responsible, whereas in her former district her supervisor was responsible for these items. She now signs her own forms and letters and has the entire responsibility for her desk. Her supervisor is there only to provide help. Laura has conducted four representative meetings (usually run by the supervisor) on various topics: One session was devoted to accounting errors, since her section was having difficulty in that area.

Laura had been a traveling relief representative, and she had no performance binder. However, she was well aware of her performance and her relationship with management. She felt she was on an equal footing with the other representatives and supervisors and that there was no formal dividing line between representatives and management. Happy with her new responsibility for service to customers, she used her own control sheet to determine her collection objectives, achievements, and flow of work. Asked whether the unit service index was important, she said it was important only insofar as it gratified management and added that her own personal objectives and achievements were more important to her.

Laura felt that she worked a great deal harder in this district, enjoyed her work more, and left work each day with a sense of accomplishment. She didn't feel that people were watching her and waiting for errors. Since the supervisor no longer checked every item, Laura felt more responsible for her own accuracy.

When asked about appraisals here as compared with her former district, she said:

> In the other district I worked very hard, but no one ever really appreciated me. Although they didn't give me the responsibility I needed, I received a great appraisal at the end of the year, and I thought I was patted on the back too much. A half hour after the appraisal, nothing was changed. I was working at the same level and getting none of the achievement and recognition I needed. I felt that the appraisal in the old district wasn't worth anything and that management didn't think much of me. Now I'm evaluated as the month goes by, and I know where I stand because I'm responsible for things. And when I make a mistake, I'm the first to know.

Reaching under her desk, she pulled out of her pocketbook an appraisal form which she was to fill in herself. She confided that she really didn't like doing a self-appraisal because it was her first time and she was a bit nervous about it. Laura said that she would probably be harder on herself than a supervisor would because she knew her limitations better than anyone else could. Since she wanted a promotion, she felt the best aspect of the district was that she had to *earn* praise here. She didn't feel this way in the other district because she didn't care. When asked how the supervisor treated her when she first arrived, Laura related that the supervisor checked her work at first, but then discovered that she could do the job and told her to make her own decisions from then on. Asked if there was one word to define the success of her unit and section, she replied, "cooperation." Everyone in the unit cooperates to give the customer good service: They all have a sense of responsibility and feel they are not only growing as individuals but also contributing something to the company and to the customer.

Lisa—supervisor. Lisa had the same organizational habits and environment as did Jane. She also thought that her function was to motivate and develop, and each of her girls kept a performance binder. An interesting item shown to us was an attitude survey sent to customers who have had recent contact with the office. (The questionnaires are sent out by central accounting and answers are returned directly to the representatives who serviced the customers.) Her reply to the question, "What does your job consist of?" was: "Motivation. I motivate my people. I was trained in class that way, and that's what I'm doing. That's what is important to me."

Lisa had heard of Herzberg and knew the basic philosophy of work itself. She does not work overtime, nor does her manager. When her group is having poor results, she selects a girl who had once been the least effective representative and assigns her the task of training the other representatives. Lisa does this because she believes that the person who has had the most difficulty in a particular area is often the one who can best explain an intricate procedure once she has mastered it herself. Lisa does not worry about customer accessibility (the ability of a customer to reach the business office) since the representatives have decided that they would like to handle it themselves.

Ted—manager. Ted has been in his present position for two years. Like his supervisors, he exercises no conventional controls and observes no quota systems on supervisory work sampling.

His major problem in the implementation of the work-itself concept was the training and stabilizing of the supervisory ranks. As an illustration, Ted told us about one supervisor who returned after an extended maternity leave. Since her supervisory experience predated the work-itself project, he faced the difficulty of indoctrinating her in the theories of work itself. To begin her re-education, Ted arranged a meeting with the supervisor and the district manager in which they discussed the theories of development and motivation. In addition, the supervisor was given some reading material on the subject, along with a questionnaire which she was asked to complete.

This was the extent of her initial training; following this session, her development was relaxed, gradual, and leisurely.

Another problem Ted encountered at the beginning of the project, in introducing the work-itself concept, was the resistance and skepticism of some of his people to the new philosophy. A few representatives were cynical about the idea, resistant to change, and unable to adjust to the new program. When he failed in the attempt to help these girls make the adjustment, Ted was finally compelled to transfer them from his unit.

Joan—representative. Joan, like most of the other representatives, kept her own performance binder and was very proud of it. In this binder was a record of the number of errors, observations made by the supervisor, returned mistakes, and her collection performance Joan is responsible for a new, growing exchange and soon began having problems with customer disconnects.* On her own initiative, she went to each section meeting and explained her problem of poor credit information. She felt that the representatives responded to her problem and that the situation improved greatly. When asked if she felt any responsibility about the problem of customer accessibility, she said, "Yes, but I feel more responsibility to take one call at a time and do the best job I can." She mentioned that she and the other representatives met together and worked out their own schedules in order to improve accessibility. Joan has led group meetings on collection and credit, and, although she was nervous, she enjoyed the experience. She has also visited the outside collection agency that handles overdue accounts, since she has most of the unit's problems in that area. When she returned from this visit, she described it to the other representatives in the unit.

Harriet—supervisor. Harriet had been a representative for two years and was recently promoted to supervisor. Although she is only 21 years old, she feels her representatives respect her even though they are four or five years older than she.

To our question about how she evaluated individual performances, she answered that she used the "sitting in" procedure. She

---

*When the customer service is disconnected, a final bill is rendered. In order to collect this bill and locate the customer, adequate credit information is needed. This is a problem of the entire unit, since credit information is taken by all the representatives even though the accounts go on the new and growing exchange.

generally sits with a representative who is reviewing her accounts, asks the representative what decisions she plans to render on various accounts, and provides constructive criticism wherever necessary.

We asked Harriet what new responsibilities had been assumed by her representatives. She informed us that she had delegated to her girls the authority to analyze all final accounts and to forward them directly to the approving authority at the fourth level, thus bypassing several levels of approval. Harriet added that negotiations were currently under way to empower the representatives to forward final accounts directly to the approving authority at the fifth level.

Another innovation for the representatives was direct communication with the manager and district manager regarding a customer's request to speak with them. Harriet said that this right was used judiciously by her representatives, and she rarely knew about such cases.

Enid—representative. Enid has been a representative for four years and has been working in the business accounts section for three months. Prior to this assignment she had been working with residence accounts and had felt bored and unchallenged. At her own request she was transferred to her present position and is now happy in her new capacity.

Enid told us that the tangible products of her work were evident constantly. When we asked her how well she attained the goals proposed by her supervisor, she said:

> Well, I suppose I care about achieving whatever goals the supervisor has in mind to a certain extent, but what really concerns me is attaining the goals I propose for myself. The reason I feel this way is that I know my own capabilities and limitations better than the supervisor does, and I can adjust my goals accordingly.

Regarding the extent to which she felt she could be creative in her work, Enid related that she often submitted suggestions for improving the job and that these suggestions were occasionally implemented. She added that, if an idea was rejected, her supervisor explained the reason.

The degree of supervision, she went on to say, was surprisingly moderate. In her former assignment, all aspects of her work were checked frequently, even some items which were very well done. "In this office, my supervisor checks only the items that I have some trouble with. Once she [the supervisor] is certain that I have mastered a particular skill, that item is never reviewed."

Enid confided to us that one of her goals was to master every job skill so that she would eventually be autonomous. She looks forward to coming in each morning and leaves at night with a feeling of satisfaction. Her only problems, she said, were her anxieties about doing an outstanding job and about advancing in the company.

*   *   *

The overall impression of the district is as follows:

- A definite atmosphere of freedom, responsibility, and accountability prevailed.
- Some supervisors implemented work-itself concepts more than others did.
- Implementation, although widespread, was strictly an individual choice and not done on a broad basis.
- Support was coming down from top management.
- The work-itself ideas were very much a part of supervisory evaluations.
- In some cases, feedback procedure was lacking.
- Employees were being given modules of work and felt proud of it.
- There was a definite feeling of cooperation.
- Representatives had no real feeling for the unit index.
- Levels of management were not clearly defined. Representatives were not in awe of the supervisor or manager and would not hesitate to talk to either of them directly.
- Representatives felt a climate of growth and looked forward to promotion.
- The approach can be unsuccessful with some people.

The results in the district, which have continued to be excellent, are summarized in Exhibit 19.

No record of talks with the district manager was compiled, for an obvious reason. A district is only as good as the people who do

Exhibit 19

OPERATING RESULTS

	Trial District			Control District		
	1966 Before	1967 During	1968 (After 8 Months)	1966 Before	1967 During	1968 (After 8 Months)
Service Index	52	78	94*	70	80	92*
Customers Not Getting Access in 20 Seconds	20.6	9.3	6.3	14.1	5.8	6.0
Resignations and Dismissals (Percentage of Total Employees, Annual Rate)	24	22	12**	47	39	31
Work Volume	.74	.78	.83	.85	.77	.81
Collection Index	92	91	94	93	93	95

* New measurement plan introduced; only three months' average available.
** This equals a saving of approximately $57,000 in training costs over the control district and of $36,000 as compared to 1966.

the job every day. It is their attitudes, performance, and cooperation that make a district what it is. It was the intention to evaluate the entire district in terms of a philosophy, and that cannot be done by listening to the top man.

What was sought was a candid and unprejudiced appraisal of a particular job environment. To accomplish this, those individuals were addressed who were directly involved in the work function. In this case, the workers did the talking and provided proof that work-itself ideas were indeed working in "A" district.

5

Insights from the Studies

E IGHTEEN FORMAL TRIALS (PROJECTS) HAVE BEEN COMPLETED, AND
the two programs in Treasury and in Virginia Traffic were
closely watched. This chapter reveals such insights as we now have
into the deceptively simple problem of work motivation. What do
we do about employees who are not producing a full day's work?
Walk over to the group and tell them to "get going"? This is often
an effective short-range motivational approach, but it is one that has
to be repeated day after day, to the despair of the supervisor and
the discomfort of the employee. What else can we do, then?

The work-itself approach to motivation, which was used in the
Bell System trials and programs, is at present an art with a good
underpinning in scientific studies. The art will move still further
toward a science as other studies are made by other people with
other insights. Our studies concentrated upon workers whose output
can be measured in order to prove that reshaping jobs according to
a definite plan could make an objective difference. Then management could decide whether to proceed on facts rather than mere
statements of feelings and beliefs. But there is good reason to believe
that the insights from the studies are just as applicable to the jobs

of bosses themselves, professional people—in fact, to the management of any employee whether his output is easily measured or not.[1]

Jobs and the Alienation of Employees

One lesson to be learned from these studies is that many jobs are inadvertently neglected, and that the job itself is often a major reason for the alienation of an employee's interest from his company. There are other reasons or combinations of reasons, of course, such as unsuitable hours, noncompetitive wages, or bad supervision. Perhaps the employee himself is ill-suited to the job, lacks basic ability, or is emotionally disturbed. But the striking reduction in turnover in some of these studies confirms the suspicion that the jobs themselves often fail as motivating factors. This is the factor that we treated as a variable, not as a "given" factor, in these studies.

The assumption was made in the studies that employees are not necessarily the enemy, nor are union officers "wrong-headed" people. On the contrary, it was assumed that the job improvement effort would be welcomed by employees everywhere, not merely by those who participated in the studies. At the moment, the judgment is supported by reactions both during the studies and afterward when the results have been reported to other groups. Not uncommonly, people ask, "When will you get to us?" This has been heard even from the men in middle management who feel they don't really run their jobs, someone "up above" does.

Motivation from Within the Work Itself

A work-itself project also assumes that (1) performance of a specified job can be much better, (2) the motivation of the workers is in question, and (3) certain procedures may correct the situation. Unless work motivation is in question, there is no need to consider job reshaping. Although the job itself must have appeal for the employee, we all agree that the surrounding conditions—the mainte-

---

[1] One project director, Bruce Duffany, says that this sentence perpetuates an inadequate point of view. He says, "We must learn to manage jobs, not people."

nance factors or hygiene—must be good or attempts at making the task itself interesting will be futile. *Employees leave for maintenance reasons too.*

Work motivation is a nebulous phrase. It is used here to refer to the attractiveness of a task or job as an employee sees it, to the employee's willingness to engage in the task simply because he gets satisfaction (that is, feels good when he does this task) reasonably often. Different jobs offer satisfaction in different amounts and at widely different times. A salesman may achieve every day; a scientist, only occasionally. Both men understand this when they elect these jobs. The impossible job is the one that offers little chance, at any time, to feel satisfaction.

Let us assume that other components of the total job environment are good. The employee gets adequate pay, the hours are good, benefits are good, he has friends at work, his boss is a good fellow, he knows that the company provides important goods or services, and so on. All the maintenance factors are fine. But how does he feel about the work itself? If he doesn't like it, don't pour on more maintenance; look at the job.

GOLF AS AN EXAMPLE

As the trials proceeded and new supervisory groups listened to the description of a unique approach—that is to say, an attempt to motivate through the work itself and not through changes in the surroundings—it was discovered that this concept is not at all easy to convey. Managers, both male and female, would listen attentively and apparently with agreement. Then a manager would seriously offer a suggestion for improving the work motivation situation such as this one: "Send each employee a birthday card with a personal note on it, rather than a routine poem or wisecrack. That's what I do and it works like a charm."

That the cards are gratefully received is not in question, but that this policy should be expected to change an unsatisfactory job into a good one for a given recipient seems incredible. That an employee who was essentially unhappy with work would start applying himself energetically after receiving the birthday card seems preposterous. It can only be concluded that the idea of motivation from the task itself had not been presented clearly.

The example of golf is useful in isolating the inner-appeal component. Golf is indeed a game, but it is also a task to thousands of professionals and teachers; as such, it can serve to illustrate the meaning of task motivation.

Neither the golfer who is out for a Saturday tour of the links nor the well-motivated employee should be visualized as going around grinning happily all the time. Any normal golfer can be expected to be angry part of the time, and to resolve never to play the game again. Yet what does it take to lead him back? A good drive, a par or two, a good final score, or perhaps a birdie.

In fact, if his score is no good at all, that alone can bring him back. He isn't satisfied with his own performance; he has internalized a standard. The simple scoring scheme gives him all the feedback he needs; he knows the facts about his success or failure.

Task motivation is clear and simple in this example. In the Herzbergian framework, the chance for *achievement* is always there for the golfer. Thence comes recognition, if he earns it. He can *grow*, get better and better, realize more and more of his potential, right up to the limits of his ability. The *responsibility* is all his. Finally, he would not be returning each week if he did not find this work interesting.

But is there not motivational power in the surround, one may ask? Does he not come for the fellowship, the clubhouse and its bar, the brisk walk in the country? Indeed he does. Yet the chances are that he can have all these elsewhere—at reduced rates, in fact! Often there are unpleasant surrounding items, such as the long wait to tee off or a slow foursome ahead of him. He is not happy about these, but he accepts them so that he can get on with his game. *The surround* is an important factor and one that may lead him to play on one course rather than another, but it is not sufficient answer to the question of motivation. The answer is in *the task itself*.

Anyone who likes games or who has a demanding hobby will understand what is meant by the motivation to work being the motivating force from within a task for a certain person. Obviously, and fortunately for the economy, not all persons find all tasks equally motivating, just as not everyone elects to play the same game. There are other good games and other good kinds of work. For those who manage jobs, there is a parallel to be drawn between golf and work.

The managers in these studies were asked to concentrate on the jobs or the game, not the characteristics of the people in them. That problem was left for the selection or employment people to resolve. The problem of picking good candidates is an endless one. However, the game can often be made more attractive for the incumbents, so that we do not lose the good people we have hired already.

In all seriousness, one's job, like golf, should provide an occasional opportunity to feel good. For example, take the Traffic operator, who answers hundreds of calls a day. Surely she should be able to have a half dozen "good shots" each day when she really feels helpful to a customer.

If so, she will come back with energy to the next call. If not, the managers must be absolutely certain that they have not deprived her of the opportunity to enjoy the job. Some comparable acts that may tend to cause turnover in the membership of a golf club or in clerical jobs are shown in the following:

Golf	*Clerical Job*
The pro follows around the course course when he thinks you are proficient enough.	Basic training continues after the girl feels she is proficient enough to start.
The pro follows around the course and makes continued suggestions about the terrain, how to play each shot, what's wrong with your body position, and so on.	Supervisory observing continues after training is over and the girl's skill is acknowledged.
The pro takes over and shoots all the tough shots for you.	A supervisor gets on the line to handle customer complaints, customer commendations, emergency situations, calls to other departments, and so on.
The pro observes you drive your new $1.25 ball into the lake, and he reprimands you.	The clerk discovers she has made an error that has affected the office performance index, and it was observed so trouble is in the offing.

This analogy illustrates the wide difference between internal and external motivation. All a manager can do is to set the stage for a good game—a good job. And there may be real limiting conditions here for the best of managers. For example, no one has yet figured a way to operate a switchboard on Sundays, holidays, and at night without manning it! Someone has to take these relatively undesirable hours. The manager does his best to assign them to people who don't mind them. The company aims to pay well and treat people well. All this is external motivation.

Then, if a job is characterized by lots of turnover and if there is trouble hiring replacements—that is, if people won't play the game—the only hope is to examine the game itself.

Must Jobs Be Glamorous?

Another example of the phenomenon we seek to understand can be found in hospitals. Why do the young girls work there, those who wear what are called candy-stripe uniforms? Or the older women in their distinctive pink, coral, or gray uniforms? Surely not for money; they aren't paid. Could it be the glamour of the uniform? Or being "where the action is"? Well, maybe.

But the presence of the volunteers (some hospitals have volunteer waiting lists) is surely not a result of either the glamour of the work itself or the pay. Some of the jobs done by these volunteers around a sickbed and in the ward are anything but glamorous. In fact, experienced workers call some of it "scut work," a most derogatory phrase.

The young girls, usually high school students, are probably working for many of the same reasons that motivate mature women whose children are now grown and living away from home. The older women may have a greater need to escape a pointless routine at home and to fill their lives again with meaningful activity. The factors in the decision that brings the individual to the hospital are probably much the same, but the weight of each factor varies appreciably from person to person. No one has written the equation or shown us the weights, and this book does not offer to do so either.

At any rate, such jobs as cooking or serving hamburgers in the hospital coffee shop, delivering mail or flowers, helping a patient with

his toilet, and wheeling a patient to or from the front door surely
cannot be accounted glamorous tasks. When asked why they work
at this job, a very small sample of such volunteers replied along
these lines:

- I was making a contribution; the hospital can't afford to pay
  everyone it needs.
- I was useful; I was helping; there was so much to do.
- I was made *so* welcome by everyone when I helped—well,
  almost everyone.
- It wasn't every day; only one day a week *at most*.
- Eventually it palled on me, and I got a different job.
- I was bored at home.

There was no explicit mention of glamorous work, excitement,
or uniforms. In terms of Herzberg's framework, the work motivators
were these:

- There is a *responsible* job to be done—care of patients.
- The chance for *achievement* is there; assignments are definite.
- *Recognition* comes immediately for the help given.
- Personal *growth* and *development* are there ("boredom" is
  an expression of the absence of these satisfiers, whether it be
  at home or on the job).
- *Advancement* to a higher order of assignment is possible if
  one has the time and the desire.

For the great mass of workers, pay is a "must"; without it, they
cannot stay on the best of jobs. But this should not blind us to the
other reasons that people work. This hospital example can be
matched by others involving volunteer fire departments, volunteer
rescue squads, local school boards, and other such organizations.
These are jobs in which people can truly have a piece of responsibility. The prize task is one that allows the individual simultaneously to
meet his needs for responsible work *and* to meet his economic needs,
needs for companionship, and so on. The level of responsibility can
be raised on many jobs. Then good pay, fair treatment by bosses, and
all the other surrounding items act as psychological reinforcers
which tend to keep people in their jobs.

Good Performance Leads to Good Job Attitudes

It has been repeatedly stated that managers need to improve jobs themselves if they want employees to have better attitudes toward their work. The entire logic of job reshaping hinges on precisely this point. Can jobs be deliberately rearranged so that people will feel productive and useful, so that the nebulous word "achievement" takes on personal meaning? When and if this is accomplished, as demonstrated in the Treasury study and its successors, good job attitudes can come into being.

In short, good performance—good productivity in a useful task—leads to good employee job attitudes. The employee is the final judge; he must *believe* he is productive. The reverse approach—struggling to improve attitudes by many other means in the hope that employees will then work productively—has not proved successful in the long run. When employee attitudes toward a job are bad, the boss should concern himself with the job and how to change it. This is the variable that has the payoff built in.

"Attitude toward the job" and "job satisfaction" are used both literally and in the restricted sense. If the job incumbents dislike their pay, supervision, cafeteria, appraisal system, tours of duty, holidays, or any other surrounding factors, steps must be taken to clear up these matters also. These factors should be distinguished as "satisfaction with maintenance items," if they are to be measured.

In short, the supervisor is stating the problem in reverse when he says, "If I could only get people interested in their work . . ." or "If only people would take pride in their work. . . ." When stated this way, a case is being made for personal deficiencies, and better employment procedures are a suggested remedy.

The supervisor should assume that, in general, new employees don't arrive already interested in the work. Even if they are to do work they have done before, they don't know how this supervisor is going to lay out the job. The carryover of attitude can be short-lived indeed. They do the job at first for one or a combination of reasons, such as money, the short commute, status of the work, long vacations, good hours, boredom with what they had done before, or purely exploratory reasons (the need to do something). Whatever the reason, if the task is well thought out and the new employee is not badly overqualified or underqualified, the stage is set for the growth of job interest, satisfaction, and pride. The job may not challenge the employee forever, his interest and satisfaction may wane, but a basically good job and a reasonably good match of the person to the job should carry him through the first six months, when turnover is so costly, and even further.

WILL GOOD JOB ATTITUDES OFFSET BAD MAINTENANCE?

Is there a risk that the case for thinking separately about maintenance items versus work items has been overstated? Is there not at least some offsetting psychological effect? It must be admitted that the answer to both questions is a qualified yes.

This answer is based on informal experience. Most people can tell of times when they endured such problems as heat, cold, fatigue, lack of interest from others, or lack of adequate help simply because their task was interesting. Perhaps by working a bit longer or harder, they could finish something they wanted to finish. Work interest and a chance to achieve—these are powerful drives that override surrounding discomforts or difficulties, especially for the short run.

A clear example of improved employee performance despite deterioration in surrounding circumstances is an emergency situation —say, a snowstorm. When employee complaints crescendo in one department of the telephone company, some old-timers pray for a storm. When the environment is at its worst, employee performance is usually at its very best. Everybody likes it. Even accidents per man-hour worked have been known to drop at a time when logic would dictate a rise.

What are the key elements in the storm phenomenon from the job motivation angle? The employee is truly needed; he knows that the community needs him and his services. His chance for personal achievement is great and immediately measurable. Service *is* out, and it is restored *by him*. Many day-to-day rules are laid aside during the emergency; employees typically have more freedom of decision. Individual responsibility is more clearly defined. These are the elements of any good job: a chance to be truly responsible and accountable, to achieve, and to be recognized for what one has done. The challenge for a supervisor is to transfer these motivating ele-

ments into the everyday job situation and to see that they are \
lost completely when the *naturally* interesting situation is ended.

A good job situation, then, may offset bad maintenance or sur
rounding factors. "Perhaps we can cut wages now!" There are two
reasons for not even thinking seriously about such experimentation.
First, if future studies support the present findings there will be less
need than ever to cut wages after a work-itself program such as
Treasury's. Productivity rose and useless steps and jobs were eliminated. The remaining employees deserve to do well economically
and share the results of a good enterprise. Anything else appears
unethical. The second reason is turnover. If several employers have
improved their jobs equally, employees will gravitate toward the
employer who maintains the best surround (wages, working conditions, and so on). One can imagine studies aimed at finding the
exact point at which employees will shift from one employer to
another. It seems a dangerous game.

The "Right Reason" for Job Improvement

The "right reason" for trying to improve the work itself for
every human being in the business is simply because he is human.
The fact that this program appears to be cost-free does not alter the
fundamental assumption. A business owes the employee the most
satisfying work it can give him within the limits of staying in
business.

Similarly, it owes the customer the best service it can possibly
give within the same limits. It also owes equitable treatment to the
shareholder, the third leg of the historic three-legged stool concept
of corporate responsibility. No business need apologize for or explain one in terms of the other. If someone protests, "The customer
and his service *must* come first," he should be asked, "How will you
render this service without employees or without shareholders to
provide the plant?" When the concept of three equally important
legs is accepted, the argument will end there.

There are times when one or the other leg may *seem* less essential. During World War II and immediately thereafter, AT&T
surely did not need more customers; it could not meet the backed-up

demand for service. In a depression, few firms need more capital or
more shareholders. And during the Great Depression, AT&T and
other industries did not need more employees. To most employees
any job was better than no job. The theory was that if you had one,
you had better keep your head down and work.

But not now! If an employee is not pleased with his job he goes
elsewhere, especially if he is young and able. That is turnover, and
the warning signal has been rising persistently.

Some turnover is to be expected and we must live with it. Employees leave for reasons such as marriage, pregnancy, illness, education, and change of location. But steadily climbing rates of voluntary resignation from valuable people who frankly say they don't like
the work is another matter. Although the figures are "messy"—that
is, all kinds of voluntary resignations are lumped with dismissals—
the fascinating fact revealed in these studies is that so much turnover
can be prevented through job reshaping.

This fallout is gladly accepted. But, as was said earlier, management owes its employees the most satisfying work that can be
provided. That is the right reason for job improvement; no other
need be offered. This leg of the stool must be as strong as can be.
People who are responsible for the work of other people in a business must never let themselves become defensive when they under-
take to utilize a man and his abilities as fully as is possible.

How One Job Factor Can Be Both Good and Bad

No one can state clearly the extent to which one job factor can
be used to offset another. Will better human relations offset a change
in the job which the employees dislike? No one knows.

As an interesting indicator of the complexity of human motivation, consider this excerpt in which one factor—money—is named as
both the best and worst job factor simultaneously. This occurred in
a taped exit interview with an employee.

> Interviewer: "Look at this from the other way. If you were
> working for the company, what would you say?"
>
> Employee: "The money. That's why 99 percent of the girls are
> working on this job. Certainly not because the job is good. I know

girls that have gotten ulcers and are taking tranquilizers, but they're staying because of the money . . ."

Interviewer: "Look at this from the other way. If you were asked to state the *worst* feature about working for the company, what would it be?"

Employee: "The money because it's too—I don't know. It's hazardous to the woman's health and her attitude and everything because it's just a curse. It really is. There is nothing terribly bad about that whole job. Nothing. You get upset and emotional and you have a good cry. But there is nothing that bad about it. It's just that it needs to be looked at."

Interviewer: (After a puzzled pause) "You said money again, though!"

Employee: "Yes, it's both the worst and the best point. The girls stay because of the money and that's bad. So you're getting phony girls."

It is conceivable that any powerful motivator such as interesting work could hold one to a job that he might otherwise want to quit if some maintenance factor such as money were poor. He could therefore account that motivator best and worst simultaneously.

Insights such as these from the experimental studies have led to the belief that survey or questionnaire studies aimed at uncovering "the most important or least important job factor" are remote and not helpful. Disputes over whether job factors can be lumped in two large groups, maintenance versus motivation, also are interesting but not very relevant—not when one factor can be rated "best" and "worst" at the same time. Also, a questionnaire aimed at learning whether either *pay* or *good supervision* is rated as more important than *work itself* seems now to be aimed wrongly. Much energy is still going into such studies.

Having established the great importance of work itself as a motivator, the boss needs to focus on improving the work itself as the incumbent employee sees it. We accept without question that a company may have no employees to study if human relations are bad enough, if it pays poorly enough, or if it has some intolerable working conditions. The market on maintenance factors must be met, not questioned.

How Jobs Become Denuded

Before presenting specific remedial steps for inadequate jobs, let us see how these jobs get into trouble.

The job of an elevator operator is a perfect example of job denuding. The first elevators had a power hoist which was run by a specialist, a stationary engineer. He sat on the ground and worked his levers while someone overhead gave him hand signals. As the equipment was improved and made safer, the operator was placed aboard the hoist. Even then, he had to be quick and resourceful to operate the steam or hydraulic lift and respond to signals from incoming as well as outgoing passengers. The job challenged him constantly.

Electricity was the downfall of challenge for the operator. (The challenge to the elevator designer remains as high as ever, of course.) No longer does the operator need to remember which floors the passengers request; the buttons do the trick in a split second. He need not jockey the cage to level it to the next floor; that problem has been removed from the job. If an operator remains aboard at all, the only decision he still makes is when to close the doors. In most modern buildings, the job denuding is total; the operator's job has been eliminated altogether.

When an operator still runs an elevator, it's safe to predict that the work itself is boring. The only choice is therefore to find persons whose limited abilities might be challenged by this vestige of the original job and find the pay level which will keep them on the job. There's no disputing the fact that the friendliness of passengers, tips, a kindly elevator starter, and similar factors might compensate a person who takes this unchallenging job. Anyone who can find people willing to take such jobs and who can live with the absenteeism, turnover, and labor disputes that go with them can count himself fortunate. But the generalization remains: There is not much *in the work itself* to challenge the operator after the first day. Young, eager people will not stay with the job—or even like it—very long.

This is not to imply that managers should stop automating jobs. On the contrary, they should go just as far as possible toward automation, especially if they can go all the way and get rid of the boring job. If unavoidable vestiges remain, they should if possible be attached to larger tasks that still have meaning and purpose. Most jobs have some boring parts to them, and people seem to accept that fact. People only dislike a task that is nearly all routine and monotony, where function or purpose is not apparent.

In a recent news account of the mounting paperwork problems in Wall Street, a "back room" clerk in a brokerage house is reported to have remarked: "I worked in a dress factory snipping loose threads, but we knew what we were doing; we could see the dress. Down here, I just check numbers, numbers, numbers. I don't know what it's all about, but it never ends."[2]

Both the thread-snipping job and the number-checking job appear to be candidates for automation in time; neither job seems very glamorous. Until automation arrives, however, one is rated higher than the other *as work* because of apparent meaning, purpose, and the sense of completing a task. Money has bought the clerk's presence, but not her enthusiasm.

The manager interested in reshaping jobs need not try to turn the technological clock back to the days before the Industrial Revolution. If he is working on an older job, he should try to think through, perhaps with the help of an old-timer, to the days when some specific job he supervises was rated a good job by its incumbents. What has been lost? Why? Did it work out in a hoped-for way in the long run? Some job simplifications and partitionings result in fine short-run gains. After the novelty of the new method is over, the neatly rationalized but simple job emerges as a problem child. Unfortunately, managers often make the error of rating the incumbent employee as the problem child.

The framemen trial reported in Chapter 3 and Appendix B is about a total job that had been progressively taken apart, step by step, until not much content was left for any one of the five sub-specialties. The cross-connection subspecialty was identified as the problem job, but the others were also less rewarding than they needed to be. Unlike the elevator operator example, however, the five parts of this job could be reassembled. Machines were not taking over parts of the job and leaving only fragments.

In short, jobs can become denuded either because of advances in science and technology or because someone took the job apart to gain certain ends which are no longer clear. Perhaps the aim was to

[2]*The New York Times,* June 13, 1968.

cut training time and costs—they should be lower for one job than for five. A new employee will be productive in only five days if all he has to learn is how to solder cross-connections. But in the long run, as the framemen trial showed, this simple job can prove quite expensive; true economy calls for a richer job.

How Jobs Are Oversimplified in the First Place

When a new work process comes along, the trained job analyst is likely to ask exactly what the steps in this work flow or work process are. The parts that cannot be programmed and automated are given to the master machine, the human being.

At this point, the unwary job analyst can lead us into a grave error. Since we are likely to need great volumes of identical parts or since a given act must be repeated over and over—say, checking a service order—we may decide to give a whole pile to one employee. "Your job is to do this and pass the product to the next person. Do it until I tell you to stop." The job is conceived as a step job. The next person adds something. Perhaps the item then goes to verification or inspection, and so on. Step jobs are not likely to be viewed as rich jobs by many people. And, if a part or paper is defective, who is responsible? Many share it, so no one feels psychologically responsible.

How else to do it? The job reshaper will go back to his flow analysis sheets and try to map out a whole module of work—a whole job, not a step. He will ask, "How much can I give this person so that he will have an entire function to perform, not just a piece of one?" To do this is a great challenge; the easy and dangerous approach is to lay out the 10 or 15 steps in a process and to get 10 or 15 people to do them one by one. Instead he should try to break the work down along natural lines or groupings of steps and assign each person all the steps for that natural block of work.

In the service order re-entry clerk trial reported in Chapter 3, the clerk's function is tied to a very modern computer. We discovered that the clerks who corrected service order errors worked much more productively and happily when five separate jobs were combined into a complete function, with each girl responsible for all five steps. Previously, each girl had only one step, which made the new job too simple and too rational. There is something wrong with giving each step to one person simply because there are large volumes of work at each step and training time is minimized when we teach each girl only one step. *Job designs aimed at minimizing training time may lead to maximizing turnover.*

"Tightening Up" As a Source of Denuded Jobs

With the best of intentions, management occasionally takes responsibility from a given job to the incumbents in a higher-level job. Take this important example as the prototype: To deny service to a customer is always viewed as a serious step in the telephone business because the customer has no alternative source of service. The most frequent reason for denial is failure to pay bills, but there are others. If the customer feels wronged, his only recourse is a complaint to his public service commission or some authority figure. If payments get mixed up or, in some way, an employee slips up, telephone service can be discontinued in error. Not only does the company regret the hardship it may have imposed, but it may have to account for its error to an angry customer and to the person (or commission) who intervened.

Suppose now that such an error has been made and that an officer of the company has been called about it. He raises a question with his subordinate, who asks his subordinate, and so on down to the person who is at fault, perhaps five levels below the officer. If at this point only one person in that chain makes yet another human error, the basic job will be denuded: If that person says, "From now on, I want the supervisors to O.K. all these service denials personally," then responsibility for not making errors is taken away from the person who does the work and shifted to the supervisor.

The cold fact is that this will *not* end the occasional error. If responsibility for this basic decision about the denial of service begins moving upward, it can easily come to rest at the third level above the employee who actually makes the denial. In fact, it has occasionally reached as high as the fifth level of management. As a consequence of the pyramidal organization of authority, this person now has to O.K. a large number of these decisions to deny service. Unless he is truly a genius he will occasionally fail also, because he simply won't have enough details and he has many other responsibilities demanding his time. Thus not only do we not eliminate error, but we may add to costs and at the same time slow service down.

These work-itself trials have uniformly resulted in returning responsibility to the lowest possible level. A generalization from the studies is this: If responsibility for a given act lies at different levels in different organizations, the odds are that it should go back down to the *lowest* level at which it is found in the organizations. And if there are selected employees with good potential even lower down, it should be sent all the way down to their level.

The trials indicate that the way to handle failure is to find the person who made the error and retrain him. But don't penalize the perfect performer, the one who did not make the error. Although the manager may be provoked, he must recognize that, by taking responsibilities away from all employees because of one failure, he is reducing the job to the lowest common denominator of performance. "Now any fool ought to be able to do this without making a mess," he seems to say. Every supervisor must accept the fact that people vary considerably in their abilities even at a given job level, and he must be prepared to give extra attention to the less able performers. He must not inadvertently take over the responsibility of the good performer with a hasty rule aimed at ending errors. That's what "tightening up the operation around here" may actually be accomplishing.

Tightening up tends to reduce jobs to the ability level of the lowest performers. An earlier point can now be restated: Jobs should not be set up at this level either, they should not be designed for the lowest level of ability. It must not be made impossible for a new, intelligent employee to earn the right to make important decisions even when some older people do not have the responsibilities. If this is done, the job is deprived of its potential richness. To some supervisors, the idea of handling employees differently may be quite repugnant; they might think it is too hard to administer the job that way. One alternative is to continue to manage in the same old way. If turnover is high and results are bad, that's not easy either!

The preceding three subsections contain many observations as to how or why jobs may have little human appeal. Some jobs lose their merit as they become fragmented or split up. Others never had merit; they were excessively fragmented from the start. Still others are denuded as a by-product of advancing technology. Finally, some jobs are unloaded because of someone's mistaken notion that the way to motivate employees to avoid error is by having the supervisor check all work. No need to worry our way through the history of more examples or to decide whether the job was born sick or reached that state later. Let us assume instead that (1) the illness, as indicated by poor results, is not fatal; (2) the job itself might be the cause, rather than the people in it; (3) jobs can indeed be rearranged; and (4) the steps toward a cure are beginning to be understood.

CORPORATE PURPOSE IS NOT INDIVIDUAL PURPOSE

In a work itself effort, one should try to separate corporate purpose or objectives from the objectives of the individual on the firing line—the person at the desk or board where a service is actually given or on the production line where an object comes into existence. When this distinction was not made in the studies, projects suffered because attention focused on the wrong problem.

The corporate purpose is to provide a service or product to the satisfaction of customers, shareholders, and employees. If we fail, the government or the workings of the marketplace will put us out of business. We may tell this story many times in an effort to motivate employees. But try as we may to sell our hypothetical elevator operator on this concept, he will see purpose only in terms of his own job. No movies, no employee communication programs, not even money will induce him to put out more effort, be tardy less often, and so on. Indeed, putting out more effort in a job like his has little meaning, little reality.

The *content*, as opposed to objective, of the employee's job is exactly the same when viewed by management and by the employee: to operate this switchboard, install this telephone, mail this bill. Both know what the employee was told to do. We expect too much when we expect the employee to give up his objective and accept the corporate purpose, for the employee has a different purpose or objective. He is looking for a chance to achieve from day to day, a chance for some responsibility, a chance to grow. It is very likely that essentially the employee *is not seeking a chance to serve customers*. This may sound blasphemous, but the serving of customers is purely incidental to achieving his end. If his job is so deprived of the job satisfaction elements that he cannot reach *his* ends, then persuasion as to *corporate* ends is of no long-term relevance. He says as he quits, in effect, "Let someone else install these telephones and do all these great jobs. I'm getting out of here."

Here again can be seen the long-term wisdom of having elastic boundaries to jobs. An employee must be allowed to grow, mature, and advance *within* jobs as well as between jobs. As he makes more and more decisions about his own task, his responsibility begins to coincide with corporate responsibility. Identifying with corporate purpose is so much easier when one has been entrusted with making the corporate decision. It will be recalled that employees earned such responsibilities one by one in the work-itself trials. And what of accountability? An employee is not accountable in any significant sense until he has an area of responsibility which challenges him. Until then, he may view himself as merely someone's "Hey, boy."

As they are now constituted, most of our jobs are designed well enough to meet corporate purpose, if only employees would make the corporate purpose their own. Job reshaping enters at precisely this point to make corporate purpose and individual purpose compatible. If the corporation fails to give good service to customers, it will be out of business. If the employee's job is unsatisfactory to him, he feels that the company is for his purposes "out of business," and he leaves it.

Here is an illustration of the dilemma as manifested in one of these trials. Eagerness to work on one purpose will block gains on the other unless the manager clearly sees the collision course. One particular third-level manager accepted the idea of job reshaping so far as could be discerned, and the project got under way. The people involved were concerned with the high turnover and mediocre technical results. As usual, the project did not move rapidly, and the manager became disturbed because employees did not show enthusiasm for the few items of responsibility they had been given. In one unit, the formal index of customer service actually slipped a bit.

In this situation, the manager launched a new program called "I believe in service; count me in." Meetings were held in which the manager reviewed results and employees were asked either to "take the pledge" that they would give superb customer service or actually resign from their jobs. No fooling! The manager said that he knew his success or failure was tied to the formal index, and he was going to "get it up." His motivational approach externally was a mixture of exhortation and threat. He planned a head-on assault toward a good technical index, with immediate results as his prime objective.

Unquestionably, he would also acknowledge a "responsibility to shareholders" as a goal, but this goal is so remote from the day-to-day problems of this middle-management person as to be properly labeled "cant"—polite and correct noises to be made in public places—unless he sees the shareholders' interest and his own effort to control expenses as an overlapping goal.

Evidently, the third goal of the business, to provide good employment, got lost in a trial aiming to improve it. Apparently this goal was actually not quite equally important. *The manager's objective*, to maintain good technical indexes every month (no exceptions), was not the employees' objective. *Their objective*, which one can infer from exit interviews, is to have interesting jobs where they can use their abilities and where they are treated as adults, not as "a bunch of school kids." Confusing management goals with the employee goals does not help the analysis of the problems of providing good jobs. The two goals may not be congruent unless a manager understands the problem and makes the appropriate moves.

The primary aim of the eager young manager, to give superb technical service, is not under attack here. His employees realize that this goal is a worthy one, but he will have to reach it through employees whose primary goal is satisfying work. In all probability, he interrupted a patient, long-term approach to one of his goals (service) when he reverted to the older motivational approaches of persuasion and threat.

A manager is usually not judged by his turnover rate. If it runs high, it is often viewed as a handicap which is attributable to the local labor market rather than caused by the manager. In our example, turnover does run high among the employees in this manager's organization, and he is operating in a difficult labor market. His motivational effort is likely to raise the rate still more because an employee can easily get a job elsewhere. This will result in more inexperience on his force—which, in turn, leads to costlier, poorer performance. Clearly turnover does affect technical indexes in the long run. When his decision to improve his index was referred to as one putting him on a collision course, the phrase "in the long run" was implicit.

Reflection stimulated by this incident and these studies suggests that top management must constantly balance customer, shareholder, and employee objectives. The man in middle management may find shareholder goals remote so far as his daily decisions are concerned (unless he senses them when he makes a move to control costs). But he must worry about the other two objectives—customer service and good jobs for employees. The manager should consider the employee reasonable if the employee seems preoccupied with having a good job, for *that is his primary goal*, just as the manager accepts a customer as a reasonable person if he seems preoccupied with having good service.

If management, by creating better jobs, finds it is giving better customer service at a greater profit for the owners, all is well. The most striking cost reduction success to date in the studies has been the Treasury effort reported in Chapter 2.

This analysis will have served its purpose if it helps a manager who suddenly finds service or costs slipping at a time when he is trying to improve the work itself. "What shall I do now?" We offer no easy answer other than to say:

- *Your* service and cost indexes are slipping, not the individual employee's.
- Don't hope to sell the employee *your* purposes or objectives.
- Avoid the usual direct approach—force and threats.
- Analyze why the work itself or the feedback from it (see Chapter 7) results in poor individual performance.
- Has some job change accidentally made the job less desirable to employees?
- Give this problem top priority in the next session where supervisors are creating new responsibilities or direct feedbacks (see Chapter 7) for the employees. What job improvements (not threats) have they to offer?

We can now say that, in general, results did not get worse initially in most of the 19 trials even though all newcomers were warned that we might have to live through such a period.

* * *

This section underscored the need for distinguishing between corporate purpose and individual employee purpose and for concentrating on helping the employee meet *his* job needs. This method puts us on the road to compatibility; films, meetings, or pamphlets on corporate goals do not. Chances are that the employee is deeply committed to serving the customer only when he is simultaneously meeting his own needs. Such an employee serves the owner well because he has been given his own little part of the business to run, not because of an attempt to motivate him from outside his own frame of needs.

6

Some Questions and Answers About the Work-Itself Approach

WHENEVER THE WORK-ITSELF CONCEPT IS DISCUSSED, MANY IN-compatible ideas emerge. The following 20 questions and answers are typical of the issues raised in meetings and workshops by management-level conferees. It is obvious from some of the questions that these conferees are concerned as much about *their own jobs* as about general management applications.

Question 1: If you hire people who are smarter than the work you want done, of course you'll be in trouble. Why not lower selection standards to get out production?

Answer: No one can argue successfully against this concept if people who meet the lower standards get out the production. As one manager remarked, "What I need is more people who are willing to come into my company, start on the bottom rung of the ladder, and stay there!" Unfortunately, the selection concept implied in this question does not really fit the facts of life. It is a simple model wherein people are viewed as square pegs, triangular pegs, or round pegs who can be sorted and fitted into matching holes—if the employment people are smart enough and if their tests are good enough.

No competent personnel test man would encourage this approach, for he knows that, even at its very best, the test approach is only relatively better than the average of the nontest approach. Test reliability and test validity coefficients are *never* perfect. One can infer correctly that people who are less than adequately qualified can squeeze through the test screen with just a little bit of luck on the multiple-choice items. Conversely, with a bit of bad luck, a person who definitely exceeds the requirements of a job may end up in a task that is not up to his ability. Thus the likelihood of high turnover remains.

Despite improved selection procedures in most businesses over the past 20 or 30 years, higher turnover rates, as shown in Exhibit 1, are substantial facts. The competent test man can say with some satisfaction, "The situation would be worse without my services." This cannot be denied. But improving selection procedures offers no bright prospect for getting out of the turnover mess.

A better model of the life situation assumes that, even if the young job applicant is precisely qualified, even if the job is neither over nor under his abilities, we still have to consider the extremely important factor of *motivation*. The question is not whether he *can* do the work, but whether he *will* do it. The ability tests indicate whether, within a certain probability range, the applicant can do the job. However, unless turnover was a criterion in the validation of the test, we have no estimate of how long he will be with us before boredom sets in and he quits. We must not assume that a person who *can* do something *will* continue to do it even though he came to the employment office without duress and voluntarily accepted the job.

A better model does not assume that excellent training alone will solve matters either. Industry and business are becoming more skilled in training a person to do his work; now we may use a highly sophisticated programmed training approach. Still one can seriously question whether this approach answers the turnover problem. As a business executive remarked cynically, "Our new programmed teaching material for that job is beautifully compact. If a girl quits before she completes it, we can mail it to her for only a few cents." Obviously, a careful job of programmed training for an unattractive job is an exercise in futility.

Most people come to the employment office for maintenance reasons. The cry, "I need a job," usually implies a need for money.

A more adequate model than the oversimplified "square peg/square hole" view of introducing the new person into the business has these elements:

- Using tests to block the assignment of a hopelessly ill-matched person to a particular job.
- Training those who are accepted as rapidly as they can learn.
- Viewing these jobs as *entrance* jobs, not as final jobs, even if applicants come in at high levels.
- Making job boundaries elastic; avoiding the "square hole" concept of a job; letting the job progressively challenge the new employee.
- Avoiding the "square peg" concept, similarly; assuming that employees can grow in knowledge, specific abilities, and skills right up to the time of retirement.

Testing personnel say a basic problem currently is that employers tend to set job qualifications too high. They like to surround themselves with competent, well-educated people. When the jobs fail to match the ability potential of the new employees, they quit. This can be the beginning of a downhill slide. Now the manager may hire more of the kind of employees who will remain at the job, no matter what their qualifications and no matter how they perform. Hiring standards for some jobs have been lowered from "college graduates preferred," to "some college training," to "high school graduates preferred," until now, high school dropouts are accepted. As part of this downward spiral the manager may even fragment the job, giving easy parts to the less-qualified people. The standards for some of the jobs shown in the turnover chart (Exhibit 1) have been through this cycle. Clearly, this approach has not solved the turnover problem.

There is the great alternative, still basically underexplored, which was chosen in these studies: upgrading the amount of responsibility in the job. If intuition and experience tell you that college-level people are actually needed, then the job should be designed to challenge a college graduate's ability.

Question 2: There is so much that needs to be done here, how can my people possibly feel underutilized?

Answer: Apparently *you* are highly motivated to get the work done, but your workers are not. How can this be? Your job can be very challenging—to keep them going, to *manage*. But they have to perform the work that you too might find below your capabilities or even downright boring. To be busy at a boring task does not remove the boredom. On the other hand, there are boring, uninteresting parts to every job. The problem is to get a favorable balance between job reward and job penalty, not to eliminate *all* boredom.

Question 3: Aren't you really, really just saying that if you want to motivate employees, "keep them busy!"?

Answer: We are not at all concerned with simply keeping employees busy. Volume of work, pure horizontal loading, is not what the work-itself ideas are concerned with. Pressure of work and a feeling of unendurable workload actually *decreased* in some projects.

This contention, that *busyness* is all the work-itself theory means, is one of the most persistent errors made by managers, especially in short presentations of the job-reshaping idea. Neither job enlargement nor horizontal loading is meant if these terms are defined to mean just more of the same thing.

Many an employee has remarked, "I like it best when I'm busy. It makes the day fly." They hate it when it's too busy, and they hate it when it is not busy enough. In either case, they are not achieving as much as they would in the "ideally busy" case which each person defines for himself. Clerks who are too busy can feel as deprived of job satisfaction as do underutilized ones if they cannot meet their own standards of a job well done. Busyness is indeed connected with job satisfaction, but it is the pace or speed component, and it was not under investigation in these studies. The fact is that pace can be a factor in a "dum-dum" job situation *or* in a rich, rewarding, challenging one. Pace may be governed simply by assigning more or fewer people to a job. A well-trained supervisor watches this factor every day. The studies in this book are concerned with something else—improving the job itself.

Question 4: But we have project work here, enough projects on the books to keep twice as many men busy as we have. Is the trick to give them out all at once?

Answer: The question of having more than enough projects to keep the workers busy is a variation of the previous questions, but it has this merit. "Project" implies a beginning and an end, which implies a chance for achievement. The assignments referred to in Question 3, on the other hand, seem to imply an endless supply of widgets to be made or papers to be processed. Therefore, the chance of a project paying off in deep job satisfaction is greater, but not certain.

The problem is set for us by remarks made in an exit interview with a third-level management man. He had supervised the preparation of all the slides and charts for three executive-level conferences in one year. That was a recurring project for him, and, he said, "I don't intend to do it again, not even once more. I'm sure I could train a sharp first-level person to do that job."

Clearly, then, this recurring project was not achievement in the eyes of this manager. His own goals and aspirations are plain to see in the title of the job he accepted in the firm that hired him away— vice president of production. He can be viewed as a prima donna, a nonteam man, or it can be recognized that a person is likely to grow in knowledge and ability, which requires that his work assignments be constantly reviewed.

A project that is dandy for one man can be a millstone around the neck of another. We persistently fail to match jobs to men, which is one of the two great challenges for a manager. The other is the never-ending challenge to keep the surround of the job in good condition.

Question 5: Doesn't the rotation of people through jobs automatically meet the need for job improvement, especially at management levels?

Answer: Rotation does not automatically meet the need for job improvement. Studies have shown that many men, perhaps as many as 50 percent, dislike rotational assignments. Those who liked their assignments were more likely to be on special projects where true achievement was possible. The other 50 percent were more likely to be those rotated among regular assignments, such as the results desk, the training job, or the practices desk.

Maintenance factors may be a real problem for the man who is rotated if the new job involves a change of geographic location. His family may be uprooted, and he may believe he is out of the mainstream and is being bypassed for promotions while he completes a routine rotational assignment.

The sum of maintenance problems and unchallenging jobs makes rotational practice questionable when done routinely. The wise manager assigns men to projects where they can grow professionally, gain greater depth of experience, make a good contribution, and then move on. Such assignments were rated "greatest I ever had."

Question 6: Wouldn't these problems all disappear if people would simply talk to each other?

Answer: How would these problems disappear if people simply talked to each other? About what? The false premises of this communication-solves-all approach are that somewhere in the group the knowledge exists as to what is wrong and that the group could fix the trouble if only its members would talk, but they won't or can't do it. Yet the fact is that an entire committee or conference of men, all ignorant of physics, will never talk itself into the construction of an atomic bomb, not in a lifetime.

A premise of the work itself approach is that new knowledge from outside the group is needed on the meaning of work. Research results are at hand. Principles are clearing up. This calls for some "telling," in one way or another.

The two approaches, telling and a working conference, can be joined. This is strongly recommended in the two-day training session described in the next chapter. The first morning can be devoted to putting in new information. Then sessions can be held in which the local experts on the work to be done are the principal communicators. Without new information, a conference calling for steps to end low productivity, turnover, absenteeism, or whatever would almost surely end with nothing more than a reshuffling of familiar solutions.

Question 7: Isn't the heart of the problem that we fail to reach the opinion molders in a group of employees, the ones who set job attitudes for the group?

Answer: Some people in a group are indeed more likely to be opinion formers than others. The solution of influencing these opinion molders, however, sounds like the worst kind of human relations manipulation—trying to entice or subvert the head sheep.

If we mean to give the key person a good job—a better, more satisfying assignment, to be followed by similar assignments for others in the group should the idea stand up under his crossfire—then this sounds like an ethical and realistic approach, one to be endorsed. In the Equipment Engineering study in Chapter 3, this was precisely the approach taken through a very outspoken engineer in the group. He heartily approved of his new assignment, which gave him specific responsibility for new additions to the equipment in 22 central offices; he talked about it to other engineers and wondered aloud why management had been so slow in arriving at this distribution of work. However, this approach was not a substitute for giving each engineer in turn a definite geographic area of responsibility.

Question 8: Surely you don't mean that job improvement applies to the work of professionals and to management people in general?

Answer: Job improvement also applies to the work of professionals within the company. The men referred to in Answers 4 and 7 are both graduate engineers. Because of their education, intelligence, and expectations, such men can "hurt worse" when given poor jobs. It is no secret that many American corporations have astronomical turnover rates at the engineering level. Maintenance factors are sufficiently similar from company to company so that the only clear reason for a large part of the shifting is the search for meaningful tasks.

Managerial jobs can be as frustrating and unrewarding psychologically as any other. And managers can have precious little freedom from pressure when any stress, such as poor operating results, arises in the organization. A manager may be told that, unless results improve, the amount of his next raise will be trimmed or the interval of time until he gets it will be extended. If the operating results are down because of his own failure to perform well, the consequence is one that he should understand and accept. The frustration comes when a manager believes that no one could have stemmed the local economic tide or whatever caused the situation and that no one could have done more than he did. To meet the command from his boss, he may feel compelled to make short-run adjustments that will eventually be costly to his operation, such as stopping all maintenance work or new construction work.

If he gets improved performance as a result of these adjustments, he is returned to the normal pay raise schedule. Thus he is rewarded for what *he* considers poor performance. In a real sense, money is not serving as recognition for a job well done when programmed this way.

For a professional outside the corporation—say, a doctor in private practice—this may mean little. He assigns or accepts work himself and has the maximum chance for a meaningful job. The full university professor who has tenure may be similarly situated, but he is likely to have many routine burdens too.

In a large private laboratory—say, those of Du Pont, General Electric, or the Bell System—the researcher in basic science is similarly graced by good work simply because he assigns it to himself. As one moves from basic research to development research and thence to engineering applications or systems engineering, the chances rise for losing autonomy. Good management then is at a premium, just as it is elsewhere in business. Can management find ways for leaving enough responsibility in any job to make it interesting to the incumbent?

It's probably safe to say that no naturally satisfying job (for instance, a professional job) is secure once the people in it form a corporation or start specializing. From that moment on, the concepts of job denuding, fractionalization of jobs, and so on all apply, and good jobs must be treasured and defended. It was an engineer himself who once remarked about his corporation, "There are a lot of good jobs in engineering here, but nobody has them!"

Unquestionably, some jobs are naturally more satisfying than others, with the operation of an automated elevator an example of one extreme and the operation of the physician's or lawyer's private practice an example of the other. They lie along a continuum. Any one of these jobs can get sick, as evidenced by such indicators as turnover, grievances, or low output. If a job is in trouble and we were to be asked to help, we would prefer that it have the potential to be satisfying, but we ought to be willing to look at *any* job.

Question 9: Are job simplification and job improvement enemy concepts?

Answer: The two are certainly aimed at different objectives, but job improvement can live with simplification. Job simplification aims to eliminate unnecessary processes; it is both a blessing and a threat to personal well-being. A person will resent being left with nothing but the fragments of what was once a rich or challenging job. Conflict between him and management is likely to result unless the simplified job can be reassigned to an employee whose lesser qualifications are suited to the new tasks.

A job can be simplified in three ways:

1. Elimination of steps or processes not needed under advanced technology. The operator aboard an almost automatic elevator has such a residual job, a "minijob."
2. Division of a whole job or process into orderly steps or tasks. These fractions are then assigned to different individuals, who can be trained relatively speedily since they need learn only part of a whole. If large masses of items are to be produced and each step requires all of one person's time, there is a strong appeal to the employer to make each step a job.
3. Movement of responsibility upward to verifiers, checkers, and supervisors.

The central office cross-connection man is an example of a person assigned to only one part of a complex task. His is a minijob as compared to that of the "combination man" in a small town telephone office. As was explained in Chapter 3, a telephone man may indeed be responsible for soldering wires together in the central office, but in the small town he may also be the man who runs the cable, runs a drop wire into the new subscriber's home, installs the new telephone, and repairs it if it fails to operate. How shall we view this paradox? Are we "against progress"?

Wise manpower utilization would view the combination man's job as follows. Any steps to simplify his job, to eliminate the "toil" part of the job are welcome. Two examples of this kind of improvement for the combination man are:

1. Use of neoprene drop wire from pole to the customer's home. This wire is noted for its serviceability and long life; therefore, fewer callbacks occur merely to replace a wire that failed.

2. Use of an automatic electric soldering gun that makes better line joints, which will require less repair time as well as less installation time.

Both these innovations are fine; there is nothing in the concepts of manpower utilization to encourage waste or toil. In fact, the combination man can achieve even more if his definition of achievement is to provide reliable telephone service for customers. That can be made a meaningful whole for many workmen.

But, if he has only one task rather than a whole service to provide, there's trouble ahead if the one task is simplified. If the automatic soldering gun eliminates the skill a man had built up and allows him only to solder an endless number of joints, then the workman can be expected to react badly. He may begin limiting production, drinking coffee more often, missing as much time as he can, and displaying all the other too-familiar symptoms of people in sick jobs.

In recent years, managers have often tried to solve this new job problem by giving the simple job to some new, unskilled employee. But, unless the employee is about as simple as his task, this does not eliminate the "goofing off" in the long run.

There is a way out—the job simplification expert must also become the manpower utilization expert. If he does not, he is potentially a mischief maker. He must be skilled in regrouping the partial jobs into whole tasks that are characterized by responsibility, challenge, and a real chance for achievement.

Question 10: Why not let the employees greenlight their own jobs? That way you would get both deep job knowledge and the beginning of cooperation toward making the changes.

Answer: One of the most commonly asked questions is, "Why not let employees greenlight their own jobs?" Some call it the job participation approach.

The employees themselves were not used as the source of new ideas in the formal projects for purely scientific reasons. The hypothesis being tested was that a job with certain characteristics produced better results than the control job. Thus employees did not participate in the redesign of the job, for then there would have been two variables, and it would have been unclear which one

—participation or the improved job—produced these good results.

Just to make sure that the fact of participation was not causing the good results, if good results appeared, neither employees nor their first-line supervisors were informed in order to control the Hawthorne effect. This may not be the easiest way to obtain good results quickly, but it is one way to find out what caused the observed effects. Was it participation in making decisions, democracy in managing a job that actually may not have been changed in any fundamental way? Or was it the result of job improvement through a change in the module, the job responsibilities, and similar things?

Job participation is a worthy hypothesis, but it went untested in these studies for a number of reasons other than the sheer scientific one. Had this hypothesis been used and had the participating employees suggested improvements in hours, lighting, cafeteria food, soundproofing, off-hours activities, supervision, company policies, or any other *maintenance* factors, the suggestions would have had to be ruled out in the tests so as to hold these factors constant in both experimental and control groups. Job participation is quite likely to produce such suggestions, and, unless management is going to truly accept them, it cannot afford to open a Pandora's box.

In fact, management might not be able to accept all the *job*-oriented items that spring out of a job participation session. Supervisors need time to decide among themselves what desirable changes to agree upon as well as the order and method of implementation. To make important changes can be upsetting emotionally to supervisors steeped in older procedures; often they have reached their present level through good performance in the older routine. Until the supervisors themselves are committed and ready for action, pressure from employees could result in stubborn resistance. Perhaps an analogy to death in one's own family is not irrelevant. There are faster ways of solving the problems brought about by a death in the family than staging a three-day funeral. But, if a family is to accept this tragic event and arrive at an adjustment, this period of time without pressure can help a lot. It was a similar need for time to adjust that led gradually to the decision that a minimum of two days should be spent on the greenlighting-evaluating process.

The allegation that supervisors may know less about a job than the job incumbents do may be true for certain individuals. However, actual sessions with groups of supervisors have not generally supported this, especially in high-turnover jobs. Experience has shown that a family of supervisors will have profound job knowledge because supervisors are usually older than their employees, have more experience, and may even remember how the job operated before it was denuded.

Another objection to complete job participation is its potential cost. One can hardly imagine stopping all employees in a vast organization for two full days of greenlighting, plus added time each week for further refinement of the list—the time requirement in our experience. A high-speed, half-day effort (or some much shorter period), involving all employees, may be a grand gesture that will not, however, result in the radical kind of thinking that was seen in the framemen trial, for example, where five jobs are to be combined eventually. What ordinary recent high school graduate would have the effrontery to put forth such a revolutionary new idea, even if he knew enough about the whole work process to conceive of it?

Next, when the implementation of items begins and supervisors know what they can and cannot do under the new plan, they can and should talk at length with employees about their ideas. Experience has shown that the supervisors know and have discussed virtually all items that employees mention.

Finally, neither job participation nor job improvement can rescue certain of the hopelessly routine jobs in many mass-production industries where there is vast capital investment and where fractions of jobs are left only because no machine has as yet been programmed to handle them. Motivational approaches to employees on these jobs may not pay off; we may simply have to live with the problem until the equipment or production line is declared obsolete and junked. A dismal outlook, indeed. Under the nonparticipation approach recommended here, at least we would not have stirred up hope in an essentially hopeless situation.

In short, the employee participation route was not followed

1. To keep the study scientifically accurate.
2. To block emergence of maintenance items.
3. To keep *job* items from appearing on final lists unless they could be dealt with.
4. To give supervisors time to think and commit themselves without employee pressure.
5. To keep the responsibility for the shape of a job where it belongs—in the hands of the supervisors.

6. To avoid the obvious high costs of two-day sessions involving all employees.
7. To avoid implying that a job could be improved when, in fact, it probably could not.

For all these reasons, let the supervisors try to improve the jobs first. Be sure to include the first-level supervisors, unless they have to be excluded for scientific reasons. Managers at all levels seem grateful for this total strategy, which avoids extending an organization beyond reasonable limits.

Question 11: How about using an attitude questionnaire to find out what the employee wants?

Answer: The usual attitude questionnaire covers such job matters as supervision, company communications, knowledge of the company and its business, pay, and food as well as attitude toward one's job. In the early 1950's, this approach to employee problems received great attention in the Bell System. Thousands of employees were covered systematically every year or two. Then the approach was dropped because not very much resulted from the surveys since the data were so broad and so difficult to interpret. The present approach calls for getting information about the work-itself situation only, and it provides a plan of action when necessary.

An employee attitude questionnaire containing only 16 questions about the work itself was used in all trials, but not as a general survey instrument. There was a small space for comments and nothing else. But it was administered *after* the supervisors had decided to go ahead with a project, not as a means of helping them decide. Thus the trial avoided stirring up employees and raising false hopes about impending improvements in jobs until there was a commitment to go ahead. At the close of the trial, the questionnaire was administered again to aid in estimating whether employee attitudes had changed. Clearly, we are concerned about the employee's own reaction. The use of an attitude questionnaire depends on timing and strategy.

Question 12: Don't you think that the problem, really, is that employees have bad attitudes today?

Answer: Complaints about bad employee attitudes are frequently voiced in the early hours of a work-itself session with supervisors.

No doubt some employees have such dim views of work that winning them over is all but impossible. However, it is false to assume that "bad attitudes" are always the fault of the person who has them.

The role of management in shaping employee attitudes was brought out dramatically in the Treasury case. When the results of this case were fed back to the newly hired women in the achieving group, one young college graduate asked repeatedly about the previous system, which had no experts, which required that someone verify all letters and sign a supervisor's name, and so on. When she realized that the control groups were actually still working that way, she remarked, "Those girls are being deprived and don't even know it."

This has been accepted as a major premise: Employees, especially the new and young ones, don't know anything about possible work arrangements except what managers have taught them. We lay out the jobs; we train the employees. Therefore, if the layout is poor, we have to fix it.

The employee himself may be a good source of information; there is no need to ignore him. But the skilled, professional exit interview with a departing employee can give us more and better insights into what is wrong with the work itself. The professional interviewer does not immediately ask, "Why are you leaving?" If he asks this early in the interview, he knows that he is likely to elicit rationalizations, well-guarded statements, or facts that the employee could not have known when he started his job search: "I'll get more money," "It's closer to home," or "I'll be working shorter hours." The interviewer centers his probing questions around some such approach as this: "Let your mind go back to the time you first started to think about leaving the company. What was going on?" (See Chapter 8 for more details on exit interviewing.)

The astute manager does not rely only upon exit interviews as a source of ideas. He may also talk informally to current employees or have skilled interviewers do it. Tape recordings for use in meetings with supervisors, made with the knowledge and consent of employees who have resigned, can stimulate new trains of thought.

Another interesting source of ideas for reshaping a job is the supervisor who has come up through that job. We can capitalize on his deep, personal knowledge of the job as it has varied over a period of years. When the job has been reshaped to maximize personal responsibility, we sometimes hear such supervisors remark: "I wouldn't mind having *that* job myself!" "Now this job is beginning to sound like the old combination man's job in a small town!" "Well, what's wrong with that? It was a great job."

The major motivator we are concentrating upon is deep within the work. If we have neglected it, we have done so only through lack of knowledge. We must not expect young (or old) employees to know what the problem is, and we cannot dismiss them by saying, "They have bad attitudes."

Question 13: What makes you think people want more responsibility?

Answer: Exit interviews indicate that there is a real hang-up or difference of opinion on the matter of responsibility. Managers think they have given employees a great deal of responsibility; employees who are quitting often feel they have had none. They have been known to say such "blasphemous" things about their jobs as these:

- They are treated like children and are told exactly what to do, what to say, and when.
- Someone is always breathing down their necks and checking to see that the work is done because no one trusts anyone else to do the right thing.
- The job does not demand any intelligence, any ability; it's monotonous and boring.

Fortunately, not everyone says such things upon resigning, but they have been said often enough to be deemed realistic.

Every job has its responsibilities. Otherwise, management would not have hired the employee who is now leaving because he has had no responsibilities. But the question is not "all or none." The question of job responsibility is a "more or less" question; how can we give this employee *more* responsibility when he feels he has *less* than he needs? The question can be phrased in such a way as to avoid arguing about whether employees have or will accept responsibility.

The evidence from the studies is very clear indeed; in general:

- Job responsibilities can be increased (no exceptions in this series of trials, but there *may* be jobs that are not improvable).

• Employees will accept more responsibilities, gratefully and willingly (exceptions may run from 10 percent to 15 percent).

Before we dump overboard the 10 percent to 15 percent of employees who may not want more responsibilities, a word should be said in their defense. When one senior operator returned the loose-leaf book in which she was asked to analyze and keep a monthly record of her defective toll tickets (long-distance calls some lucky customers may have gotten to make free because of the operator's error), she said, "You keep the book. You always have." Management has taught many older employees that error analysis is management's job, not theirs. The senior operator certainly rejected the responsibility when it was offered, but only 2 other girls out of 23 in that particular office did so.

Finally, no one can say whether this operator will still be in the same frame of mind a year from now regarding this issue or whether she will reject a different item of responsibility when it is offered her. It is likely that a refusal is a way of "getting even" and not a final statement of how things will be in the future. The supervisor in this case requires a great deal of patience; she needs to clearly understand the goal of job reshaping. Job improvement through the work itself is a never-ending process.

Question 14: What *does* the supervisor do if he is not a work pusher, checker, and disciplinarian; won't he feel lost?

Answer: What will the role of a supervisor be under this new procedure? A supervisor in one of the projects answered this question for us when he said, "At last I've learned that it's not my job to do the employee's work. That's *his* job." He went on to add that the supervisor's job is

• Scheduling the workforce.
• Training.
• Continuing training.
• Turning new responsibilities over to employees as they prove able to carry them.
• Counseling or consulting on job problems.
• Counseling on personal problems.
• Planning for the handling of new kinds of work.

- Informing employees of changes in company goals, objectives, and problems.
- Helping employees to relate their goals to company goals.
- Planning for the elimination of unnecessary tasks.
- Relating his work to the processes that go before and after so that the flow is smooth.

The supervisor must, in addition, take care of the surrounding or the maintenance items. This is always extremely important.

The above-mentioned supervisor added, "At last I find that *I'm a supervisor* of the work. I'm not one of the workforce, and I wouldn't go back to the old way for the world." The support of the *lowest* managerial levels in these projects has been one of the strongest bits of evidence for the general decision to continue with a program.

Question 15: In a way, aren't work-itself projects just a way of getting bosses to change their style of management?

Answer: What *is* a boss's style of management? Will a work-itself project change that style? An analysis of styles of management and an attack upon them seems to take us toward a no-man's-land where nothing happens. If we have between 12 and 20 bosses at a work-itself conference, we can rest assured that many styles of management will appear. Some bosses are more authoritarian than they should be. Others may be more democratic than is wise in a complex, technical work situation where degrees of knowledge and skill make people quite unequal. This denies the wisdom of a "one-man, one-vote" philosophy in a work situation. Some bosses are quite insensitive; others may be excessively concerned about employee reactions. Some are endowed with a charisma, which has helped them up the leadership ladder; most are not.

Rest assured that there is no agreed-upon concept of an ideal managerial style. Some social scientist, somewhere, can be found to favor *any* position, from tough-mindedness at one extreme, to an employee-centered position that relies heavily upon individual motivation at the other extreme. Since there is no agreement as to the *style* the boss should have, there is little purpose in determining which conferee has how much of what *sort* of style.

If the problem of changing the work itself is cast in terms of defective styles of management, we are obliged to try to specify:

1. What styles are present at the conference? To what degree?
2. What style do we *want?* To what degree?
3. How do we change a manager's style?

This whole approach seems hopelessly complex; it takes us deep into personality analysis and theories of personality change. It asks, "What's wrong with the boss?" and is thus essentially negative. It is a "punishing" approach; much time will be spent in teaching the conferee that he is a hopelessly antiquated character. If the training or conference is oriented this way, many a conferee will spend all his time figuring out how to survive intact until the conference is over, even if it necessitates taking an oath, so to speak, that he will reform when he goes home.

In the next chapter, the training material purposely avoids accusing or attacking the conferee, his ego, his pride, or his person since the usual reaction to accusation or attack is denial or counter-attack. Instead, the conferee should be provided with the latest information as to what great numbers of employees seem to want. They want "More Than a Living" (to use the title of a film in the AT&T training series). The conferee should have an opportunity to check his knowledge and understanding of the work-itself philosophy through several stimulating written tests. A greenlight session can stimulate his creativity in applying these principles to the work processes under his own control.

Those who have directed the projects discussed in this book agree that many supervisors need to change very little or not at all *in their style* when they reshape the job at hand. Others need to change quite a bit, and some of them cannot do it.

In any case, one must conclude that the problem common to all the conferees is a particular job. Analysis of styles of management has not been helpful in deciding what changes to make in the work module, the work flow, or responsibilities for the completion of a job.

The style of management of some bosses may change as a result of the projects. Many bosses say their outlook on other people and on life in general has been affected. As one phrased it, "This is really a quiet revolution." If so, it was achieved by concentrating the conference time on the way the job is set up, the way it runs. If this is inadequate, and if the boss joins us in changing it, that's good enough. Character analysis is unnecessary.

Question 16: Professor Herzberg's work has been both criticized and applauded. How do you look at it?

Answer: First, let us present the applause for Professor Herzberg. His basic text, *The Motivation to Work*,[1] has proved to be a powerful stimulus to research. There is no question that it was the fountainhead for this series of studies, in which one factor (maintenance items) was held constant while the work motivation factor was varied. The results are in line with Herzberg's predictions; striking gains in job attractiveness resulted (see Chapters 2 and 3). We are learning how to help supervisors work with this important variable. Deserving applause, then, are two points:

1. The way the theory focused on an important and frequently neglected variable (the task).
2. The way in which the theory provided a simple framework for conveying the message to those who would be asked to do something about the situation (the maintenance versus motivation theory).

What is the criticism? Mostly it is that the theory oversimplifies a very complex situation. One should first note that the very *purpose* of a theory is to simplify a complex situation; in fact, the simpler of two theories usually gets the nod in a scientific dispute if it can account for the experimental facts as well as does another, more complex theory.

Upon what, then, is the charge of oversimplicity based? Here the argument becomes hard to follow. The difficulty is that the critics are not producing countertheories that account for experimental facts better than does Herzberg's. His work has stirred up enormous productivity. But the studies, with few exceptions, are also of a survey type, done by using questionnaires or some methodologi-

---

[1]Frederick Herzberg, *The Motivation to Work*, John Wiley & Sons, Inc., New York, 1959.

cal variation, rather than using Herzberg's approach through personal interviews. Sure enough, differences sometimes result.

As an example, the authors of one interesting article point out that in their questionnaire study of 600 aerospace workers, men sometimes thought pay would be more important than achievement in a certain situation. The authors conclude, however, "Motivators are more important to job satisfaction than are hygienes (maintenance items), this importance being on the order of 3:1."[2] One shrugs his shoulders.

Unfortunately, then, the flow of critical articles is still generally at the first of the following three stages, with virtually no work being done at Stage 2 or 3 where the need is great.

> *Stage 1.* Survey in which employees are asked either to remember or to guess how they did or would feel under certain conditions of employment.
> *Stage 2.* *Experimental-simulated* work groups in which people (usually students) are divided into control versus experimental and are asked to perform work of some kind (Tinker Toy construction, anagrams, and so on) under various "treatments" or conditions.
> *Stage 3.* *Experimental-real* work groups in an ongoing, living situation, as in the studies reported in this book.

The critical articles seem to say: "Herzberg developed his theory after a Stage 1 study. He might not have arrived at it if he had used a different survey approach—ours, for example." This is hard to deny, but it does not represent an impressive advance in the understanding of work itself as a motivator.

Another criticism of Herzberg's work alleges that his two group factors, maintenance items and work motivators, are not independent. Not much work has been done *experimentally* to check whether the theory is right or wrong. The present experiments started with the deduction that work itself would be a strong motivator when maintenance factors are constant. This turns out to be the

[2]C. A. Lindsay, Marks, and Garlow, "The Herzberg Theory: A Critique and Reformulation," *Journal of Applied Psychology*, Vol. 51, No. 4, August 1967, pp. 330-339. For an analysis of such studies, see especially D. D. Whitsett and E. K. Winslow, "An Analysis of Studies Critical of the Motivator-Hygiene Theory," *Personnel Psychology*, Vol. 21, No. 4, 1967, pp. 391-415.

case, but some contend that satisfaction with the work itself is affected by the fact that it is paid well or poorly. It is a "subtracter," one might say. In other words, there is an interaction effect. A man may like the work (say, the ministry), but he hates the low pay; so he likes the actual work of marrying, christening, and preaching somewhat less well.

These are interesting and potentially useful speculations. In the meantime, Herzberg has provided a practical framework for management training even if his two factors prove to be correlated in some way that no one has completely specified yet. This is not without parallel in other human situations: There is a strong positive correlation between the two human factors of height and weight, yet they are quite separate concepts. It is a good idea to know both when buying clothing.

Similarly, Herzberg's separation of the employee's total job into two separate groups of factors was a happy one. It clarified thinking and, in the case of this series of studies, pointed a way forward. Herzberg has urged experimental attention to the work itself as a motivator while pointing to the necessity for keeping maintenance factors under control as potential dissatisfiers.

The authors of an exhaustive review of more than 80 research articles bearing on managerial motivation arrive at essentially this same point. In their concluding paragraph, they emphasize that the time has come for experimentation. That they speak of managers rather than employees does not seem a crucial matter.

> With the exception of the study by Herzberg *et al.* and some of the recent work of Porter and Lawler none of the other studies reviewed attempted to probe the question of the effects different motivational patterns have on managers' performance or work behavior in general. What is needed is a treatment of managerial motivation as the independent variable and measures of performance as the dependent variable. Experimental designs may be more suited for this type of research wherein certain motivational variables can be manipulated experimentally while controlling for other variables.[3]

[3]L. L. Cummings and A. M. ElSalmi, "Empirical Research on the Bases and Correlates of Managerial Motivation: A Review of the Literature," *Psychological Bulletin*, Vol. 70, No. 2, August 1968, pp. 127–144.

Question 17: Are you trying to change human nature?

Answer: People who ask if we are trying to change huma.. usually take a dim view of human nature, at least as displayed b, others. They usually imply that the situation is hopeless; change is impossible, not worth attempting.

These studies are based on the hypothesis that human nature is not spelled out and rigid. Therefore, it can be modified or shaped differently; plasticity is the keynote. The great amount of change revealed by the studies indicates that this must be correct. The results can be traced to changes in performance, and the changes in performance result from a series of work-itself steps based on some fairly new assumptions about what people want.

Human needs as we now understand them must be met. We also have an obligation *to develop* the human resources within the business. Now that the studies and programs are well along, it is possible to link the work-itself effort to not less than six major ideas about man, his nature, and his behavior that have been developing since World War II. Here are the ideas.

1. Herzberg, Maslow, Argyris, and many others have stressed the human need for *a meaningful piece of work*. Otherwise, life lacks richness, and, especially as America moves toward an economy of abundance, the individual who is aware of this lack will struggle to get out of the situation. The work-itself approach has managers load the job with all the desirable human stimuli possible within practical limits—limits which are far beyond what one may think at the start of a project.

The next few ideas linked to the work-itself concepts were suggested in a report by A. H. Brayfield,[4] executive officer of the American Psychological Association, to a Senate committee on development and use of human resources. He said he finds the word "motivation" a bit esoteric and troublesome, so he turns the issue on this question: How do we *shape* human behavior so that a person—any person, whether deprived or not—can acquire the skills and habits that lead to the rewards that sustain the behavior? And the idea that behavior can be shaped implies that human nature is quite plastic.

2. According to Brayfield, the most powerful tool in shaping

[4]A. H. Brayfield, "Human Resources Development," *American Psychologist,* Vol. 23, No. 7, July 1968, pp. 479–482.

behavior is *selective or differential reinforcement* of the desired response. Much work in the area of operant conditioning has been done following that of B. F. Skinner at Harvard. In the work-itself approach, first of all the job should be laid out as elastically and challengingly as possible; then the employee in that job should be rewarded *positively* (not punishingly) for his successes. Negative responses may serve to stop undesirable behavior, but desirable performance results most readily from positive reinforcement. As employees show more and more competence they earn more new responsibilities or privileges, the big reward being the right to make their own decisions about many phases of their particular assignments.

At this time in most corporations there does not seem to be any practical way to use money as the immediate, day-to-day reinforcer for the majority of employees, but money is only one of the possible rewards for work successfully completed. Satisfaction with the work one does and the outcome of this work is a daily reinforcer if handled well.

3. The *manager's expectation* is another powerful factor in shaping behavior. Within the past few years, a striking report on research has become available which shows that the expectation of a teacher, for example, greatly affects the behavior and accomplishment of the student. The work of Robert Rosenthal[5] of Harvard showed dramatically that, when teachers were told that certain children were ready to "spurt ahead" intellectually, the children did just that, even though it was known that they were no more gifted than the other children in the room. Note that the gains were in *measured intelligence*, not merely in stored knowledge. Rosenthal concluded that more attention should be focused on the teacher than on the pupil in educational research if we want dramatic improvement in pupil performance. Those who believe that human nature is fixed should pay particular attention to Rosenthal's work, for few traits have been thought to be more firmly fixed than intellectual endowment.

The work-itself studies dealt principally with young adults rather than children, and the measures of improved performance are quite different from Rosenthal's. Furthermore, the focus was on actually

---

[5]For a brief summary, see *Scientific American*, Vol. 218, No. 4, April 1968, p. 19.

improving the basic tasks, not merely the supervisor's perception of them.

But there is a link. An effort is made to change the supervisors' perceptions of their employees and what they can do if motivated and freed to do it. In our work-itself workshops we devote considerable time at the outset to a discussion of what employees seem to want (the Herzberg structure). Our film, "More Than a Living," is an example. Although some supervisors may view this approach with skepticism, most management people *in our experience* agree with it. One function of the workshops and visits is to encourage and to *reinforce managers* in their new view that many employees *want* to do more than they do, that they *can* do it, and that operating results will actually improve if supervisors act on this set of assumptions. We capitalize heavily upon this way of shaping employee behavior by trying to change the managers' expectations.

4. *Employee participation* as a way of shaping behavior had substantial support in research since the work of Kurt Lewin during World War II. The people who took part in his studies became committed through participation, and personal satisfaction and improved morale resulted from their acts. The work-itself approach deliberately plays this down, but only in the belief that employee participation *comes later*. First, management must be persuaded that something good can happen if the work itself is changed so that the module or slice of work is maximally meaningful.

Once that is over, once the greenlight items are agreed upon and the program is under way, the work-itself approach might be viewed as going *beyond* mere job participation to the *final* making of decisions within the agreed-upon areas. The job should be given to the well-qualified person, just as completely and finally as possible. That is the work-itself approach.

5. *Ideas, insights, and thoughts* can act as strong shapers of behavior. They serve as internal stimuli linking bits of behavior together in a reasonable way and increasing the probability that, when behavior is called upon and needed, it will be relevant and consistent. The workshops and the follow-up meetings aim to provide the basis for shaping behavior in this way. Greenlight sessions and other devices are avoided if they are substitutes for a clear understanding of the ideas that generated the list. People are discouraged from "borrowing" someone else's list. When new job problems arise

—and arise they do week after week—the manager who has helped make a list has a framework for checking the consistency of a decision. Even if he realizes that the task that must be done or the step that has to be taken is not loaded with internal work motivation, at least he may be able to soften the blow by acknowledging the fact.

To date, craft and clerical employees have not been consulted about the ideas behind work itself as a motivator. Therefore, the idea does not shape their behavior except as it is mediated through the bosses.

6. Unlike lower animals, man can simply watch something good—or bad—happen and decide that this new and personally untried behavior is something that he also wants to do—or not to do. The persons who were involved in the observed happening serve as *models:* One does not have to be hit by a truck to know, vicariously, the terrible consequences. In the work-itself approach, employees who perform well receive more freedom to perform independently. As the studies have shown, many of these people move on to better jobs. This is a practical application of "modeling" for those who have not been given the desired responsibilities as yet.

In at least these six ways the work-itself effort can be linked to the school of thought which believes that human nature is malleable and that its manifestations can be changed radically. If a critic holds, nevertheless, that human nature "away down deep" is unchanging it can only be said that, for practical, useful purposes, the opposite position is a better one.

Question 18: We have "human factors" men. Don't they look into this sort of thing at the stage when equipment is being designed?

Answer: Many observers say that human factors men do not consider the work itself when equipment is being designed. Their job is usually to see that pieces or configurations of equipment *can* be used conveniently by average employees. They ask questions like this: Can an employee run this typewriter with spaces of this width between keys which offer this many grams of resistance while averaging fewer than X errors per hour?

But we are raising a long-run question: *Will* he continue to do it? This question may force us to inquire into a *total* work process. Is the employee viewed merely as someone who types or keypunches whatever someone else brings him? In the design of total work systems, human factors men must see the vast social responsibility which is theirs. Then they are less likely to think of themselves as physiologists or physiological psychologists alone and may also see themselves as social psychologists and humanists, concerned not only with what an employee *can* do but with what he is *striving* to do with his life.

Question 19: Why not hire consultants and get an outside point of view?

Answer: A consultant can be of great help in starting a series of family sessions. If you are short-handed or lack expertise, consider hiring help. If you are short of money, consider using a knowledgeable headquarters man; he may be able to play the valuable role of "outside helper."

Frankly, beware of proposals to "make a study." Very often these are only delaying tactics. If you think a particular job can be helped, use the approach outlined in Chapter 7 to "study" the matter. In two quick days, you may have a good answer. We agree you'll probably need help, but not many consultants are as yet skilled in or even conversant with this approach.

Question 20: What criticisms could you make of your own work?

Answer: The main criticism of our own work would be that the approach may sound easier than it is. There must be careful attention to the details of implementation. Precisely when and how will these steps be taken? Who says what to whom? Why?

A number of people have to be concerned, such as a project or program director, the top bosses who can shoot the whole thing down easily and accidentally, and the new, uninformed supervisor who replaces someone in a location where a project or program has been going well.

Similarly, union representatives need to understand and believe us when we say that this is truly meant as an effort to give employees *good jobs*, not fragments of jobs which underutilize them and their abilities.

After a hasty reading, someone may take shortcuts in the patient greenlighting approach. Changes may be introduced without supervisory backing. Other changes may have no substance. Some may be downright errors; for example, if maintenance items are labeled motivators, programs will fail. At one location, after the boss heard of these studies, each girl's picture was placed over her work station

orn hope that this would make her more responsible for
customer contact.

erent criticism is that the studies presented here do not
nufacturing lines or processes—places where there may be
enormous capital investment and where changes in human effort
may be harder to visualize. There is work to be done, but we do
not believe the manufacturing situation differs in its essence. If job
specifications have been written for the jobs in a manufacturing
location and agreed upon in union contracts, the road will admittedly
be longer. But better jobs are to be found along the same road in
all cases.

There is no doubt that Herzberg's basic theory will be changed,
amended, or modified in time since that is the nature of science.
This statement is hardly a serious criticism of the present work; it
is merely an acknowledgment that perfection is never achieved.

The area where one feels most impotent is that of recognition—
a great motivator in Herzberg's theory. In other theories of learning
this has been called *reinforcement, feedback,* or *operant management.*
Whatever the label, the area needs study in order to do this well
for employees.

Supervisors are not alone in seeking to learn how to handle this
aspect of life better; parents also feel inadequate here. Just one current book, Haim Ginnott's *Between Parent and Child,* was on the
New York Times nonfiction best-seller list throughout 1968. Ginnott's book purports to help a parent develop good relations with
a child by reinforcing good behavior rather than by punishing bad.
This is anything but a new idea, yet his book presents detailed
things to do and not to do, to say and not to say. A similar work for
supervisors based on hard evidence, not anecdote in this area of
weakness, has long been awaited.

Finally, there is not a variety of solutions to offer. The next
chapter offers one "prescription," the single survivor of many that
were tried. A few early approaches were simply buried before the
19 trials began. For example, representatives of four companies were
called together and told how to fix the keypunch job in Accounting.
They were told clearly and well, but were not helped to find items.
Not one trial ever really got off the ground as a result of that meeting. But others will come through with other good prescriptions in
due time; this is only a starter.

7

The Art of
Reshaping Jobs

EARLIER CHAPTERS WERE DEVOTED TO FINDINGS AND CONCLUSIONS in AT&T alone. This chapter presents possibilities for job reshaping in a way that meets the challenge of John W. Gardner when he says, "Too often we give people cut flowers when we should be teaching them to grow their own plants."[1]

How does one get started? Would it be best to set up one test project, a few projects involving jobs, or a program? A *project* has been defined as a scientific study complete with experimental and control groups, efforts to control the Hawthorne effect, reasonably large numbers of employees in measured jobs, and so on. In a *program*, any supervisory group may get the training and knowledge. The effort is talked about freely. Measurements are much less formal; success or failure is gauged by comparing current results to those of a comparable period a year earlier, two years earlier, or whenever.

In the hands of an experienced manager, such data may be quite meaningful. If turnover drops 10 percentage points in one city in

[1]John W. Gardner, *No Easy Victories*, Harper & Row, Publishers, Inc., New York, 1968, p. 68.

his territory, he can interpret the drop in the light of his knowledge of the labor market in that city during that period. Take a real example from a program. One manager felt that possibly half of the improvement in the turnover rate was due not to the work-itself effort, but to a mild business recession. Jobs in the city were harder to find, and perhaps fewer employees quit for that reason. If one must be certain whether the work-itself experiment is a success or a failure, the best method is to set up a formal project wherein randomly selected parts or units in a city or plant or building are designated achieving groups and others are held out of the program as controls. Then, at the end of the study, one can compare the turnover data from the two groups for this time period without so much worry about outside effects.

Each person who undertakes a work-itself effort for the first time must appraise his own situation and make his own decision, of course. But enough is now known that coherent evidence for it can *and should* be presented to the top administrative people. They will then be in a position to decide whether to specify *projects* or *programs*. Two big benefits emerge from this:

1. The responsible person can add his "blessing"; if need be, he can protect the infant project or program.
2. If one administrative head decides not to enter, he nevertheless has an informed basis for cooperating with some *other* department that has decided to go ahead. He knows what it is striving to do and will not accidentally "shoot down" an idea for improving a job.

Such meetings with executives generally take two or three hours. The meeting can follow this general outline:

1. Presentation of the basic idea (that work itself can be a great motivator).
2. Presentation of data to support the idea with persons present, if possible, who have participated in earlier projects.
3. Question-and-answer period.

The leader of the meeting may not want to press for a formal decision and a commitment at this time, especially if the meeting is interdepartmental.

WORK WITHIN A DEPARTMENT

As an outcome of this interdepartmental, administrative, or executive meeting, at least one department will probably ask for a trial project or program. The leader might want to suggest that the start be made with *one* major job.

If this is agreed upon, a work-itself workshop should be arranged. Several natural families of supervisors should be present at such a workshop; a supervisory family is defined as several levels of bosses who share responsibility for the job that is to be improved. For example, the bosses of a given group of service representatives in the Commercial Department are (1) the business office supervisor (lowest supervisory level), (2) the business office manager (Level 2), and (3) the district commercial manager (Level 3). The division commercial manager (fourth level) and the general commercial manager (fifth level) will also certainly want to sit through the working sessions a time or two.

A reason for this control over the composition of the meeting is the greenlight session (often called brainstorming or creative thinking) mentioned in Chapter 3. Unless they are naturally related, there is no meaningful way to greenlight several jobs simultaneously. It was possible to work on toll operating and on information services simultaneously because they are varieties of the same operating job in one department. Similarly, joint meetings were conducted for the management people of several different central offices when the basic job under consideration was the same. At first, the conference should be limited to 12 people. Later on, larger workshops of perhaps 15 to 20 conferees may be practical.

A workshop where several families are represented should be divided into natural groupings to work on the greenlight lists. The groups may use separate rooms at the same time late in the first day. If the jobs are related or are part of the same work flow, the groups may want to discuss the possibility of reassigning job duties and responsibilities when they reconvene on the second day. However, if there are only a half-dozen conferees representing two or three related jobs, the leader may want to keep them together and greenlight the jobs one at a time. *Stimulation from other people is especially important* in the early stages.

Clearly, then, the meeting of top-level people should be interdepartmental and the actual greenlight sessions strictly intradepartmental. Since specific decisions can affect several departments, this interdepartmental meeting may avert real conflict. For example, when a red light glows on the wall over certain calendar dates in many telephone business offices, no service representative may agree to give service to a customer on that day regardless of urgency unless she obtains the signature of a supervisor. The red light is turned on by the Plant Department when it estimates that it has a full workload for a particular day. In nearly every trial, this was viewed as an unwise restriction on an intelligent, well-trained girl who is faced by what she considers to be an emergency in some customer's home. The right to override the red light was viewed as a responsibility to be earned.

Yet the Plant Department rightfully has a voice since it has to install that service on that particular day—it will almost certainly have to arrange for overtime work or premium pay. Department heads who have participated in sessions on job reshaping have been able to work out the necessary details in this instance. Below the executive level, however, the greatest strides can be made by keeping the greenlight sessions within departments.

The Problem of Commitment

Commitment lies at two distinct levels. The lower-level management people will certainly not want to carry out even the best of the greenlight items unless they feel sure of executive-level support. As was discussed earlier, executive commitment is essential.

But this commitment alone will not sustain a job improvement program or project, nor will ordering suffice. Once they are assured of executive interest, the lower levels will become committed through the analysis and evaluation of their own greenlight items which occur on the second day in the work-itself workshop. If a group is not satisfied that *considerable* good can be accomplished through their own items, the project or program should be quietly dropped. This rarely happens, however.

The question of commitment, to do or not to do, should be clearly raised and clearly answered. While there is no need for haste, a few days should be ample. If the answer is yes, the project should be transferred to the group. The leader then begins to act as a consultant and to provide counsel on follow-through.

PICK A PROBLEM JOB

In the project stage, the focus was on either a problem job or a job that had not been running as well as its managers wanted. Management jobs, staff jobs, jobs held by only three or four people, and similar positions were avoided because the results are usually not viewed as "hard" data. Even if successful, the project would therefore not convince many people. Eventually, however, these jobs may call for improvement also.

If this approach is adopted and the right projects or programs are selected, the gains will be obvious and the same procedures will be acceptable in jobs that are less easily measured. By this time, the work-itself procedures should be well in hand.

Some jobs are fundamental to a business; all others support these basic or building-block jobs. In the telephone business, these jobs occur at the interface between customer and company. Some examples are—

1. The service representative or marketing representative who sells the customer the service in the first place.
2. The installer-repairman who visits the home or business of the customer and places the instruments.
3. The traffic operator who supplies information and connects calls upon request.
4. The engineers and the plant men who arrange the facilities for connecting one customer with another.
5. The people who do the billing and collect the money.

These are the kinds of jobs on which to work. If a key manager is unhappy and puzzled with his current operating results, he should stay away initially from such jobs as those of the janitors, the food purveyors, and those in personnel and public relations. These are supporting players—who are, however, essential to smooth operation and must be reached eventually if their positions are characterized by turnover, absenteeism, high costs, and so on.

As an attention-getter, it is often said, "Job improvement starts at the bottom." This is an antidote to the usual complaint that all new programs should begin with the president, proceed to the vice presidents, and then move on down in orderly fashion. The management jobs in almost every trial changed in some important way as a result of improving the interface job. Some levels actually disappeared (see the Treasury study results in Chapter 2 especially). But interface jobs cannot be abandoned; that is part of the definition. What a waste of time it would have been to improve the verifier's job in the Treasury correspondents' trial, only to find later that the job itself was no longer needed!

The *program* director especially will find that supervisory groups will want to greenlight other jobs on their own once they have worked on an interface job. A *project* director may want to restrain them so that the demonstration study group does not become uncontrolled. For example, in changing the information operator's job, no changes should be made in those of the service assistant or group chief operator unless they are caused by the basic change in information operating.

Job reshaping should start with the basic jobs simply because they *are* basic. Changes there force changes at higher levels. In not one project has the work-itself approach resulted in the addition of more layers of control.

Finally, in any large corporation there may be more jobs needing rethinking than can be covered in formal program sessions. The idea is to *really* help every management person just once in a formal way. From then on, as he thinks about his secretary's job, his one stockroom man, or his two building maintenance men, he should be able to chat with the program director or manpower utilization man informally.

A Suggestion for Calling the First Workshop

Once a crucial job has been selected, a two-day workshop should be arranged with the families of managers (first through fourth levels) who are responsible for getting the work done. Every effort should be made to isolate these groups from their daily jobs and interruptions and get them off the premises if feasible.

If a job is really in trouble, expect there may be resistance to removing supervisors even for two days. On some occasions supervisors were so completely involved in day-to-day fire fighting that they declared themselves unable to take time out in order to start over. "Wait until we overcome this shortage of trained people. The employment office says things will be better soon. Then we'll start." This is exactly the problem that job improvement hopes to help solve; a workshop is not a sunny-day vacation.

Consequently, one needs to help managers, especially at the lower levels, find time for a meeting. On the occasions when we settled for what few supervisors we could get when we could get them, the project did not turn out well.

Once they are at the meeting, the managers should be encouraged to leave the responsibility for running the job with an acting supervisor. Here is an example of what can happen. A severe equipment "outage" or failure occurred in one of the trial traffic districts while all the supervisors were attending the work-itself workshop. Service assistants had been left in charge. The managers involved talked the situation over and decided *not* to rush back to their buildings. By the close of the conference (the second day), the service assistants themselves had called to tell—with great pride—that they had managed the situation *themselves* and were carrying high service loads.

Prospective conferees are expected to read or to work out in advance the following four items:

1. "Reaction to Your Job,"[2] a set of 16 questions which conferees are asked to answer and which they can use to test their own employees' job reactions *before* the trial begins and again at its conclusion.
2. Form A of a test, "Work Motivation Basics."[3]
3. One of our completed studies, especially the Treasury study.
4. "New Approaches in Management Organization and Job Design."[4]

Other items come along for consideration as preconference material from time to time. For example, some groups have profited

[2]Copyright, Frederick Herzberg, Case Western Reserve University, November 1965.

[3]This unpublished test by AT&T for Bell System use consists of 27 agree-disagree items, each of which proposes a good or poor work motivator.

[4]Frederick Herzberg, *Industrial Medicine and Surgery*, Vol. 31, No. 11, November 1962, pp. 477–481.

from Professor Herzberg's "One More Time: How Do You Motivate Employees?"[5] Local project or program reports might be suitable so long as they do not overwhelm the supervisor. This entire book, for example, is too long for preconference assignment for the work-itself workshop. The conferees should be allowed to perform individual tasks in advance, thus saving conference time for establishing a common base and performing the common task—revision of the job in question.

A word of advice about using old greenlight lists: Don't! If an accounting group plans to work on a keypunch job, for example, don't provide a list of items worked out for some other keypunch group. This tends to make "cripples" of the supervisors. Furthermore, it could make a project or program degenerate into a mere routine attempt to adapt one man's solution to another man's problem. To use John Gardner's analogy, it would be giving cut flowers to people who want to learn how to grow their own plants. Their supervisory situations will change with time. They need to know the *how* of greenlighting and its basic concepts so that it can be applied in any situation at any time. They do *not* need pat answers to pat questions that are useful only in working with imaginary people in hypothetical situations. This book is intended as an outline of an *exercise* in problem solving, not a "crib sheet" or "pony" of solutions. There is no harm in using a few *illustrative* items from greenlight lists for a few familiar jobs, but *none* should be offered for the job that is being worked on in that particular group session on greenlighting.

PROBLEM CHILDREN AND PROBLEM WORDS

The words that stand for "motivators" are at so high a semantic level that no one knows precisely what they mean. If you see a package on a shelf above your head, you can recognize some things about it from the sight of no more than two corners and an edge. If the "something" appears to be rectangular, you can estimate the total number of corners and edges and the size based on previous knowledge of rectangular objects. Unlike visible and tangible objects, "responsibility" is an example of a high-level word. When does

[5]*Harvard Business Review,* January-February 1968.

an employee have some of it or enough of it? What is the "package" like? Could it be that enough responsibility for one employee is not enough for another with greater ability? Can an employee who is challenged by a certain job this year grow out of it in a year or two?

Unlike the package on the shelf, responsibility is shapeless and unbounded. Similarly, other long-term motivators—achievement, advancement, growth, interesting work itself, recognition—have unclear meanings.

These problem words lead to problem situations and problem employees. If managers fail to recognize that an employee is inadequately challenged, attitudes start to slip. In the past, managers have tried to improve employee attitudes through movies, discussions of company objectives and the employee's part in them, and similar programs. Now it is becoming clear that, unless the work itself is improved, the attitudes will not improve. Attitude is generally a result, not a cause. The change in measured attitudes of the young women in the Treasury case is experimental evidence in support of this statement.

One can see the similarity in the psychological growth of children. If a child is taught to play the violin or work algebraic equations skillfully—granted some native endowment—he becomes interested in the violin or in algebra. Interest generally *follows* success in learning. If there is nothing in his environment to challenge his learning ability, a child becomes bored. Children like challenge, in amounts that vary with physical conditions, intellectual ability, the distractions of competing activities, and many other factors. Success in meeting the challenge—achievement—is the basis for good attitudes or interest in the situation. This is but a slightly different restatement of what has been called the motivating force in the work itself.

BRIDGING THE GAP

Operationally, the problem of improving the motivational situation boils down to this: How does one move from such mind-numbing generalizations as "recognition," "achievement," and "responsibility" down to the work itself? The answer lies in the two-day work-itself workshop with its greenlighting session where the precise plans for the "bridge" are shaped (see Exhibit 20).

Exhibit 20

BRIDGING THE GAP IN THE MOTIVATION OF EMPLOYEES

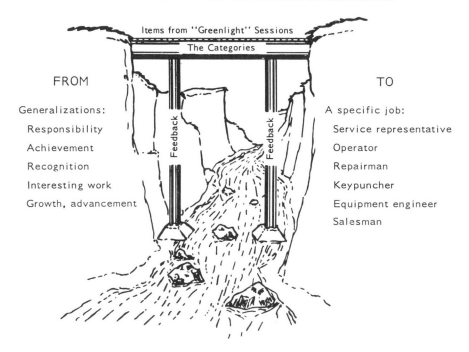

In the greenlight session only two of these generalizations are emphasized—the *inputs:*

1. *Responsibility.* How can increased responsibility be loaded into this particular job (the vertical concept, not just more of the same task)?

2. *Achievement.* Can responsibility be assigned in such a way that the employee can have an obvious achievement, something that he himself has clearly accomplished?

The other two generalizations are the *outputs:*

3. *Recognition.* At first the employee is greatly dependent upon the boss and others, but eventually he will himself recognize when he is performing well and will be pleased if management has built in feedback devices so he knows others recog-

nize good performance too. This is the desired internalized state. Such motivation is truly from the work itself and, as such, is the goal of the effort. The boss should continue to reinforce good performance, of course, but the motivator is built in.

4. *Growth and advancement.* If a job is laid out ideally, an employee will have a progression of tasks and skills before him. Those employees with ability will grow faster and will soon need a chance for advancement to a higher level. Some jobs —medicine, research, top management—have a lifetime of challenge in them.

The challenge to management is to lay out jobs flexibly for people of varying abilities at all levels so that they can enjoy work and achievement as much as the professional man does.

The Work-Itself Workshop Meets

When the family of management people responsible for a group of employees is assembled, activity is distributed approximately into two days:

The first day

1. Make a list of personnel problems that confront the conferees.
2. Discuss the idea or theory behind the work-itself approach to solving personnel problems as opposed to other methods (movies, discussions, and updating of formal studies). (1½ hours)
3. Review one or both test instruments, "Reaction to Your Job" and "Work Motivation Basics," as a check upon specific understanding. (2 hours)
4. A free-association greenlight session in which the supervisors, without fear of criticism, sarcasm, or the "dead hand of the past," toss out ideas for giving employees more responsibility, recognition, growth, or whatever. This session is seldom completed by dinner time of the first day. All items are recorded on large easel-pad sheets which are hung around the conference room.

There is no evening session. However, the group is encouraged to stay together informally. A statement expressing the thought in the following dialogue is the only "homework."

> Perhaps you have heard this quip?
>
> The "Conservative": "I don't think we supervisors ought to be trying things for the first time."
>
> The "Moderate": "I disagree. We should indeed be trying things for the first time. But not now!"

What we ask is that you think radically about the work flow and the jobs involved. Be "radical" in the surgical sense, as it applies to an operation that cuts deeply to a root cause. Don't worry—yet— about the actual "operation." We will perform it conservatively once we know what needs to be done, for a radical operation on a human or a radical change in an organization can be fatal if undertaken care- lessly. What *could* be done that would result in more complete jobs for employees? First thing in the morning we will finish off any greenlight items. The price of admission in the morning will be two greenlight items or one very good one!

The second day

1. Open the meeting by presenting another view of where work motivation lies and where they should concentrate the greenlight effort.

   A. Supervisor →   *B. Employee* →   *C. "Customer"*
                                           The work-itself area

   If there is day-to-day satisfaction in a job, it lies between points B and C, between the employee and the "customer" (the product or service). In the area from A to B lie the rules, procedures, and human relationships that facilitate or hinder. This is the main- tenance or support area, always in need of thoughtful review. But the final search for enriching items should center upon the area from B to C. Eventually, but not immediately, the group may want to hold greenlight sessions to enrich the supervisor's job, which is represented by the area from A to B.
2. Continue greenlighting. (1 hour)
3. Begin evaluation (the redlight session). (3 hours)

A. If the greenlight list is short (up to 50 or 60 items), the group can work as a committee of the whole in assigning each item to one of these categories:
   (1) Change of *module.*
   (2) New *responsibility.*
   (3) New form of *recognition or feedback.*
   (4) A *growth and advancement* item.
   (5) *Roadblock*, a rule or procedure that should be eliminated.
   (6) *Maintenance* item.
B. Most items will fit into more than one of the first four categories under A. The leader can list such items in several categories or ask that each be channeled into the category that best describes it. An item is not likely to be one of the first four and also a roadblock or maintenance item.

   If the list is long (more than 50 or 60 items) and conference time is growing short, the same category list is used but one or two persons are assigned to each category. The person or team should then walk from sheet to sheet, marking ("branding") the items in the assigned category.

   Assign each category to a conferee (or team) and ask each to mark on the sheets a rating for each team, as follows:
   ** This one seems like an *excellent* idea.
   * This one seems pretty darn *good.*

   Each person or team should now list on a clean easel sheet:
   (1) His double-asterisk items.
   (2) His single-asterisk items.
The remainder (the redlighted items in this scheme) can be written out or listed by number. They are thus painlessly classed as "not-so-great" ideas. The leader is well advised to ignore them from then on, lest consideration of them eat into conference time.
C. Ignore whimsical items and deliberate shockers.

4. Each person or one member of each team reports on his list his judgment of its strengths and its deficiencies. Occasionally, the reporter will come through with a new idea at this stage, but

this is not typical. For the first time, conferees are being asked to state whether their part of the list has merit. The project or program shapes up at this stage, especially if the first four categories under 3A are strongly represented.

5. If the list is strong on *roadblocks* but weak in the four categories, there may still be the basis of a program but not such a healthy or constructive one. This combination suggests a basically rich job that has become hemmed in by rules and regulations. The group should discuss this possibility. Is the alleged fact indeed true? Is this a rich job that has become blocked?

6. Maintenance items certainly deserve to be segregated on an easel sheet also. Two treatments should be considered:

   A. If a *program* is involved, this question should be discussed: "Why don't we fix at least these double-asterisk items? Who should or will take the responsibility for listing them, programming action on them, and following through?" If maintenance is bad, it can be disturbing to a program.

   B. If a *project* (experiment) is under consideration, the maintenance items must be changed in both experimental and control groups or not at all. In the trials, it was generally recommended that they not be changed at all. This was because the trials were testing the notion that changes in work-itself items, not maintenance, were *strong* motivators. The opposite hypothesis is also open for testing. Some social scientists, in fact, contend that maintenance factors are strong work motivators too—that an employee gets pleasure from them, enjoys his work because of them, and increases his output as they are increased. For the time being, such hypotheses are not considered as productive as is the work-itself hypothesis.

7. If two or more groups have greenlighted separately, each group should make its own report to the conferees. To hear reports from other supervisors in related jobs can be stimulating and encouraging.

8. Implementation should be a general topic if it appears that a

project or program is in the making. Just how does a group go ahead? What should it do next?

   A. The leader briefly summarizes for the conferees the steps and material included in Chapter 8.
   B. Families separate and work for an hour on three or four of their meatiest items, outlining in parallel columns on easel sheets (1) what problems and obstacles each item entails and (2) how each might succeed.
   C. The leader comments on each item, emphasizing that if such an approach is taken *item by item*, the conferees can open the final door in the search for better jobs.

9. Commitment is obtained. If possible, the meeting is turned over to the highest line-management person present, and the group decides whether a job improvement trial or a program is to be undertaken. The top person selected should have been quietly forewarned just before the groups report. (30 minutes)
10. A tentative, short-range timetable is outlined by the top management person and his supervisors, with the conference leader as a friendly adviser. A four-week interval is usually about right, a period wherein the greenlighting, the evaluating, and the laying of plans for implementing good items continue. There should be active discouragement of the quick start which is frequently desired by an enthusiastic group. At best, the family groups should meet two or three hours per week until ready to actually start. If groups greenlighted separately, they may continue to meet separately. That is, only those who have quite similar problems should work together.
11. End of conference: Usually 4 P.M. of the second day. Some may feel it unnecessary to spell out these steps in such detail, but anything short of this may result in the waste of two days.

SOME FURTHER THOUGHTS ON GREENLIGHTING

The greenlight process goes by many names: creative thinking, wild thinking, and freewheeling, among others. There is no reason to think that the sessions will be at all "wild" or that they call for great bursts of creativity. The latter concept, in fact, seems a bit pretentious. AT&T workshop leaders settled for the simpler, more neutral notion of greenlighting; that is, don't stop the supervisor for any reason when he is trying to think of ways to load responsibility into a job for an employee. Later on his ideas will be evaluated. This approach has paid off very well to date, but some other schemes might work equally well.

If the leader is knowledgeable about the department whose people are greenlighting, he may be shocked at some of the practices which conferees suggest as the roadblock items. The leader may have thought such practices were out of date, antiquated, even primitive. Yet they are still here! In this situation, the leader can destroy his own workshop by becoming defensive and telling conferees that the item is not necessary since the situation is outmoded. He must accept (for working purposes) that the supervisors know what they are doing on the job and that a proposed change is a real change for them. He would do better to simply go along with them and use this information to help top management know what life is *really* like at the craft level.

Confronted by a long list of ideas—probably anywhere from 15 to 115—the newly appointed leader may have two feelings: (1) This is too much and (2) not many of them look meaty. He must learn not to expect a wonderful, "meaty," obviously good, brand-new idea to emerge. It has happened a few times, but this is not likely in a job that has been around a long time. Rather than seek *one* world-beating idea, he should instead help the managers find the *group* of ideas which may possibly make up one very good idea.

In labeling items as maintenance, a flexible viewpoint is advisable. Later in the process, the leaders may want to restore those that can be considered "facilitators," items that are truly linked to a work motivator. For example, it was decided to strike off two items: "Print calling cards for the telephone installers" and "Put their names on the truck doors." Later these items were restored because the foremen decided to give each man his own truck and his own group of city blocks. It was judged that name cards and names on the truck doors would encourage the men to identify with the customers. For other jobs, such as keypunch operating, the printing of name cards might appeal to vanity or a sense of security; this is not motivation from within the work itself.

Within such a category as "new responsibilities," the conferees may find some clear subcategories. As an example from the telephone installation trial, six basic groups of items could be identified concerning

1. Care of trucks, loading of trucks.
2. The worker's route from customer to customer.
3. The worker's responsibility for the quality of his work.
4. Direct personal contacts with customers.
5. A geographic area (from the modular category).
6. The worker's progress or growth as a knowledgeable telephone man.

A subject of great interest has been the lack of interest displayed by any one management group in the items generated by some previous group even when the job involved is the same. The few times such a list was offered late in the second day, it was likely to be discarded in a few minutes as the group returned to its own business. The conferees didn't criticize the list, but they implied that other managers could not possibly have as relevant a list of ideas as their own. This is actually true, for the same telephone job—for example, that of the installer—is quite different in Manhattan and in a rural community. In fact, there are real differences in Manhattan alone between districts composed of apartment houses and those composed principally of office buildings. Therefore, greenlight lists are always attached to a place and a time, even for a given job. No longer is it suggested that a new group of conferees look at an old list.

HELPING MANAGERS TO GREENLIGHT IDEAS

Unless the leader is reasonably conversant with the job under consideration, he may want to get away from the easel after two or three items—that is enough time to get the greenlight session going. He should give the crayon to a highly knowledgeable person who knows the shop-talk of the supervisors and the rules of the game, but the group should not be deprived of one of its most fluid thinkers by making him secretary. And, of course, the leader doesn't relinquish his role, and he should step in if the proceedings slow down too much.

In either case, the leader or an appointee must work quickly at the easel without the interruption of long explanations for the benefit of anyone in the room. Here are some rules of the game:

1. The conferees may ask each other for small items of clarification, but there should be no long explanations at this point. If it is explained that this comes later, in the redlight phase, the participants will cooperate.
2. Some conferees may block the flow of ideas when they offer comments such as these: "Won't work." "We tried that back in 1965, and it failed." "Are you trying to be funny?" "Oh, please; not that again." These purveyors of gloom should be diverted diplomatically but firmly. The cold fact is that old-time failures have on occasion turned out to be good ideas for new times in a new context.
3. No magic target or quota of items should be provided but there should be no hesitation to tease the conferees with "You can do a lot better than that" or "I've seen longer lists."

WHAT IF A GREENLIGHT SESSION FAILS TO TAKE OFF?

It has been observed in various trials that some jobs are so potentially rich that proposals for vertical loading simply poured forth. On one particularly productive occasion, 116 items were produced easily; of these, no more than 10 were dropped in the first evaluation session.

But what if the supervisors have great difficulty in coming up with ideas? On several occasions when this has happened, it was found that the job was so restricted that it truly could not be improved as it was. Only when the supervisors decided to collapse two or three separate functions into a single job was it possible to formulate ideas for a good, improved assignment. This has been a major and exciting find. We may stop a floundering greenlight session and tell the supervisors, "Perhaps you should consider combining two or more related jobs. Is it possible? What happens before and after this person does his part of the job?" Note that this probing for details does not contradict the previous injunction against offering greenlight items. If and when the meeting quiets down too much, the astute leader will be prepared to say, "Have you been thinking about this or that part of the job?" But he will not offer his own items.

Exhibit 21

A SCHEME FOR THINKING ABOUT IMPROVING WORK ITSELF

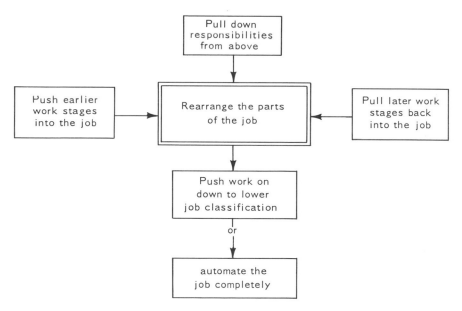

A way of thinking about job improvement is diagrammed in Exhibit 21. The following questions should be asked:

1. What does the supervisor now do for this person that he could do for himself once we are sure he is competent?
2. What steps that now precede his work should be *part* of his work if he is to have a meaningful module?
3. What steps that are now done after his work would make his module more meaningful and responsible?

4. What tasks should be pushed down to a job at a lower level of classification?
5. What could be automated completely?
6. Was there once a way of handling this work that was more meaningful or satisfying in some respect?
7. What do we let an employee do in an emergency or in the absence of his supervisor that he might be allowed to do all the time?
8. Can accounts or customers be divided into meaningful classes (all TV or radio accounts, all department stores, all hotels, and so on) so that an employee might be given responsibility for a certain type of customer?
9. Are there any verifiers or checkers who might be dropped?
10. What training could employees give each other? What specialized knowledge might they be encouraged to build up? What new things could they learn to do that someone else now does?

If a job cannot be improved, the personnel department should hire only those people whose ability levels are so low that they might be challenged by such a job. All that is needed is "good enough" ability; this is not the kind of person we expect to see move up into management. If a person has been hired with more talent than the job calls for, then we must move him into other work. As for those whose abilities were correctly appraised, who are good enough and that's all, not all of them will be happy at their work. Some will be disappointed because life (and the company) permits their friends to rise while they do not. Some may quit. The work-itself approach does not envisage wiping out turnover, but it certainly is aimed at slowing it down. All the more reason for trying to see that current jobs are as full as possible of responsibility, and a chance for achievement and for recognition. The goal is to retain workers as long as possible.

The Problem of Visitors and "Brass"

A less frequent cause of a slow start by the family of supervisors is the presence of visitors or observers. Their presence is often easily justified; they may be planning or thinking about a program of their own. And there can be no question that the single most persuasive item is the work-itself workshop session. Nevertheless, the presence of visitors may inhibit the greenlight session; much depends upon who they are.

Visitors, in general, can be handled easily: Tell them, gently and with your most disarming smile, to sit around the edge of the pond (not at the main table) like good little frogs. Then tell them that they may croak but only with permission or upon command! This should end the problem.

Officers and high-ranking departmental people in the family present quite a different problem. However, the leader can capitalize upon their presence. Find a moment to speak to them alone. Tell them that they may think of greenlight items as the session develops, but ask them to delay offering suggestions until they feel that a definite lull has occurred. Suggest that it would be most helpful if they led off with the *most provocative* item that has occurred to them, not the most innocuous. Tell them that the aim is to capitalize on what the group knows. Warn them, too, that the least secure supervisors will be watching them out of the corners of their eyes for signs of alarm and that they should act like good poker players for a bit. If they find themselves under observation, they should wear faintly encouraging smiles. This approach may result in a richer pot of usable items, no problems, and a far better session.

In large organizations which have many family groups, the grapevine will be in operation. If upper levels of management do not attend *all* of the meetings, the conferees will have precise knowledge of how they *did* react during earlier sessions! Do not be surprised to find middle and upper management dropping in on every workshop. In the statewide program for the telephone operators' job in Virginia, the fourth-level managers not only came to every meeting but were obviously the masters of ceremonies. The conference leader was quite clearly helping them. They played a subsidiary role once the meetings started, but they were real towers of strength and purpose. In addition, the department head for the entire state (fifth level) dropped in on many of the meetings and did not once fall off his chair with alarm. If the job in question is at all improvable, then this approach is unbeatable: The conference leader or program director should act as the knowledgeable person and consultant, with the upper levels doing their normal job of counseling, supporting, deciding as the program proceeds in the organization.

One can hardly prove the case with a single incident, but those present during the first day of the difficult framemen trial (Appendix B) believe that its success was partly due to the full-time presence of the department head (fifth level). In fact, when the conference leader was called out of the room during the greenlight phase, the department head himself took the crayon and wrote items on the easel sheets at the direction of the conferees. His demeanor was all the "come on" that was needed. No speeches were necessary. In the closing hours of the conference (when commitment is the issue), he led the conference again.

THE SEARCH FOR A MODULE OF WORK

The natural module of work is an elusive but a key concept in making work more meaningful. Here is an actual example that came to our attention at the outset of these studies.

A group of ten girls were responsible for getting out any charges in toll bills on staggered dates through the month:

> Exeter 2—due out February 1
> Exeter 5—due out February 8
> Exeter 7—due out February 13
> Exeter 9—due out February 17, and so on.

The girls worked as a team: When they finished Exeter 2, they started Exeter 5 under the scheduling and direction of the supervisor. But productivity was bad, due dates were missed, costs of overtime were high, and so on. A young college graduate on one of his first assignments saw the answer: Give *one girl* responsibility for getting out Exeter 2, another girl Exeter 5, and so on. She might or might not have to get help from another girl. In either case, each girl in rotation had a *whole* piece of responsibility—all of Exeter 2 by 5 P.M. on a specified date. She had to organize the effort and succeed or fail by herself. Although this was not a controlled experiment, the results were viewed as dramatically good. A girl did not have more work to do, merely more of the say about the work she was going to do anyhow. (It also proves that the greenlighting phase can be done by one person, if he knows what he is doing. After participating once, many supervisors are able to go on alone to another job under their responsibility.)

Previously the billing task had been automatic. The supervisor's orders amounted to: "Work on this pile of papers. When you are done give them to her. Then we'll bring you more. We'll tell you when to stop." Thus accomplishment was hard for a girl to see.

A natural module in the telephone business might be an exchange or all of a certain class of work arising in a district, which is always composed of a number of exchanges. A still larger unit is the division. In telephone station installation trials, foremen laid out city blocks and assigned them. This brings many allied problems, but this natural module (in this case, a geographic area) is a valuable concept. Following are applications of the modular idea in our studies; remember, however, that each is only the first change in an allied series.

The Job	*The Module*	*Old Approach*
Station installer	All installation work in certain city blocks, parts of town.	Follow a route set by someone else.
Frameman, toll office	All framework, equipment assigning, and final circuit testing. Turn over to customer.	Complete frame cross-connection work only.
Service order re-entry clerk	All four or five steps in correcting errors on orders rejected by the computer; follow until order is correct.	Find and correct the error but don't work on additional changes necessitated by correcting the error.
Keypunch	All cards from certain geographic areas or for certain kinds of reports.	Whatever cards need to be punched next.
Equipment engineer	Handle all contacts from initial request to final installation in a certain area or for certain kinds of equipment.	Whatever job came along next in the entire company.

Not all jobs worked on are listed here. In every case, we seek to give an employee a feeling that he has a place—a customer or a set of customers—all his own. For an engineer, the customer can be either someone else in the telephone company or someone outside. Each employee feels that

1. He has a meaningful task, one he can describe. ("I handle all work on _____ for this district.")
2. His responsibility is clear. ("If I don't have this circuit up and working at 4 P.M., the football game won't be relayed through.")
3. Achievement takes on meaning. ("I did get the circuit up by 4 P.M.")
4. He receives recognition from *himself* as well as feedback from his boss or the customer. ("It worked well and on time. I know.")
5. He has all the responsibility. ("Yes. They depend on me to have this done when we promise the job. If it isn't, I'm the fall guy.")

The results from a modular approach can be almost unbelievably good. Here is a report precisely as a craftsman wrote it about his work in his new "private" territory, his "Block 42." The project had been running only three weeks when he wrote this report, without any suggestion from supervision. Only his name is omitted. Remember that this project was begun because operating results from the men who install the telephones, maintain the condition of the plant (poles, wires, safety features), and deal with customers were less than satisfactory in this area.

PROGRESS REPORT, BLOCK 42, BY ED—STATION INSTALLER

In general. I have made several inspection tours of my area in an attempt to seek out any extraordinary plant violations and to decide where immediate attention in the area is required. So far, I've seen nothing so bad that I cannot continue to work my area as I have been doing. Service order activity in the area has been light, enabling me to devote most of my time to outside plant.

Work done. In the past two weeks I have worked on four streets in my area: Ellsmere, Stanley, Spaulding, and Genesee (between Venice and Airdrame). With the exception of Genesee (on west side of street), this section of my area should be completely free of outside plant violations and defects. Time in this section has been spent placing and removing hardware on poles where needed, raising and rerouting drop wires, and dressing up pole terminals so they'll look neat.

At the houses I've tightened any loose insulated drop wires, re-routed drops that were too close to power, replaced or remounted any loose attachments, and corrected other minor defects. Although all protectors in this section have not been checked, the ones that were checked were either already converted or converted by me.

House visits. In this section of my area, I've made several house calls, just for the purpose of introducing myself and acquainting the subscribers with our new program. (This has been very beneficial.) It's made the subscribers whom I've talked to aware of what we are doing—and they love it. It's also helped me to seek out any inside telephone defects, such as insulated wire coming away from walls, twisted 25-foot cords, and so on. On two streets, I shot three cases of trouble and handled four complaints; I even taught one of our customers how to adjust the bell on his telephone. None of these cases of trouble or complaints had ever been reported.[6]

Work not done. I have not replaced any ground wires, as I feel they can be replaced after all violations of the new state code have been eliminated. And I cannot honestly say that all protectors (fused type) have been converted, but they soon will be. There are a number of trees and bushes that need trimming; those that were not trimmed by me have been turned in to construction.

This is an up-to-date report as to what has been going on in Block 42. I plan to make a report each month until my area is completely clear of outside or inside plant defects. I'd like my fore-man to inspect the section mentioned in this report and give me his opinion of the quality of work I've been doing, his comments, complaints, or ideas.

[6]Some responsible plant administrators question the economic feasibility or wisdom of letting Ed—— perform this unrequested house work. This should not lead us to conclude, however, that Ed should not do other items or that the new plan be discarded. Rather, the management problem is how to channel the interest of this highly motivated individual now that his full energies are being released.

Meeting the Block: "Too Costly"

In the evaluating sessions, greenlight items are often rejected because of expense. Take trucks as an example. Since not every man on a force of 100 telephone installers is at work on any given day, we may need only 85 trucks. Illness, personal problems, and vacations all contribute here. Conceivably, then, all trucks could belong to a pool, be loaded identically, and then be assigned one at a time to the installers as they got their work orders for the day. The dollar savings would be substantial.

Despite this logic, one of the first greenlight items regarding installation was, "Give each man his very own truck." Foremen know their men want this, yet cost computations will be cited to kill the suggestion. It is necessary to remind everyone that turn-over is costly, too. The decision to shoot down or retain any green-light item must rest upon its contribution to the solution of our major problem, job dissatisfaction. If the item provides a substantial base for increased responsibility or enhances the likelihood of accomplishment, then the item must *at least* be given a chance in a trial program at some test location. The truck problem has not yet been resolved because the evidence is not all in. It is used here merely to illustrate the work-itself approach.

Offsetting the costs of extra trucks might be the costs of employee job dissatisfaction and turnover, such as—

1. Hiring a new employee (several hundred dollars).
2. Training him in basic electricity and in installation (more than a thousand dollars).
3. Repair and waste owing to his lack of skill (unknown amounts).
4. Bad customer relations owing to the inexperience of the workforce (impossible to estimate).
5. Absence (impossible to estimate).

Turnover is a problem in all major departments. In Chapter 1, discussion was restricted to resignation and dismissal (excluding death, retirement, and transfer, which are relatively uncontrollable). The following table points up, for a few major jobs, the great amount of hiring that must go on to cover turnover *for all reasons* in a large corporation:

	Traffic Operating Force	Service Representatives	Plant Men
Employees at start of 1967	190,000	27,000	222,000
Hired during 1967	90,000	21,000	33,000
Net gain (loss) end of 1967	(28)	700	2,700

That is a lot of hiring to maintain the force and achieve the small gains shown on the bottom line. Remember, too, that for every person hired, eight or ten may be processed through the employment office. No manager faced with a bad resignation and dismissal component in his total turnover situation should accept this as a normal cost of doing business unless he has tried and failed with a work-itself effort.

FEEDBACK MUST BE INDIVIDUALIZED

At the very first greenlight session, encourage the supervisors to come up with ideas for giving job incumbents the feedback for personal performance that is not yet available and is so important.

Observe first that the group results and indexes have limited motivational appeal to those who actually produce the results. Such indexes measure the effectiveness of the supervisor in his dual job of maintenance man and job designer; they do not show the results of any one employee. Mistakenly, we too often depend upon the public posting of our deficient results as the means of causing employees to reform and perform better.

So long as the case is put to them in terms of *group* pride—company objectives, district goals, campaign or contest goals—the motivating power (if it exists at all) is outside the employee. The reason campaigns wear out or fail in the first place is that the motivation is *our* motivation as supervisors, not the employees' motivation.

When the going gets really rough and the pressure is on the lower levels for better results, motivational techniques may become still more primitive:

1. Managers may threaten to withdraw maintenance factors completely (in plain English, to fire someone), but this adds to the ever-present turnover horror.
2. They may then resort to "TYE," or thumb-in-your-eye. We never do this physically, of course, but often we do it psychologically. We threaten, hound, and harass the poor performers, those who are tardy or absent, those who perform only at the bargained-for level.[7]

Let us go along with current predictions that the last third of the 20th century will see greater shortages of competent employees than ever before in U.S. history. Therefore, attempts to motivate through thumb-in-your-eye techniques will have less and less chance of providing good operating results, because any competent young person will simply leave. The best indicator of this will be the under-six-months' turnover rate.

What is the answer, then? It bears repeating: Make the *work itself* as interesting and meaningful as possible. Share responsibility until workers are well trained, then give it to them. Let the employee's chance for achievement be his motivator. On the strength of these trials, the case for this approach cannot be denied.

This logic dictates the necessity for finding meaningful ways to let each employee know how he is doing. Not the office index, but his own index. Not the workload that the office is carrying, but his own part. Not the office sales quota, which was met only 87 percent, but *his* percentage of *his* quota, be it 100 percent or 50 percent. The bridge diagram (Exhibit 20) shows feedback as the piers, the supports which make the bridge safe.

To get individual feedback items requires ingenuity, but it certainly can be done often. In the service representative trials, the record shows 16 ways of giving a representative her own performance results, which were previously available only on a group basis, if at all. As another example, take the case of the station in-

[7]For a full description of this approach to motivation, see Herzberg, "One More Time," *op. cit.*

staller who was given his own set of city blocks. As a result, a whole set of figures became available for him, all referring to his area; so far as he was concerned, this was something new in his job. Generally, and surprisingly to some observers, this feedback notion does not decrease what might be called control data; it increases the total amount, for now the employee has his own.

Like one's own golf score, these personal results can motivate an employee to perform better. The average golf score and par for the course may be of interest to the golfer. Similarly, office results or district results may be of interest to the employee; but they are not as meaningful and personally motivating as precise knowledge of his own performance. Why? His own score reflects his own length of service, his own difficult territory, or his own dexterity or mental ability—all of which he must live with daily. If every golfer played the same golf course, average scores might mean more. Even then it would still be necessary to know how long he has been playing, his physical condition, his equipment, and so on before we could judge his performance.

Insofar as employees differ in service, ability, and personality, and insofar as they are up against different customers or different physical conditions, they must be given the means for plotting their own progress.

If greenlighting is the practical way to bridge the gap between such *general words* as "responsibility" and such *specific acts* as assigning each engineer his own central offices, then items of *feedback* become the piers that hold up the structure. Without individual feedback, soundly based recognition cannot be given by the boss, nor can the employee give it to himself. In other words, he cannot say to himself with certainty, "I'm doing a real good job now compared to last month." The beginner needs to hear from the supervisor how well he is doing, but the experienced employee should be reasonably independent. This internalized state is the goal. This does not mean, now or ever, that the boss can abandon his employees once he has set up some good direct feedback devices. He still should talk with even the best of performers about performance and about goals.

8

Following Through
to an Improved Job

How do you keep a job improvement program alive once it has been put into operation? This chapter explains how to do this in detail, because a work-itself program cannot persist without some week-to-week supervision. The forces of habit are against it: As soon as some stress arises, old solutions are trotted forth. But the AT&T studies have shown that job improvement certainly can survive quite well with moderate attention.

An Implementation Schedule

The following schedule is a good framework for a work-itself program:

1. *Getting support—interdepartmental*
    (a) Schedule officer-level information sessions aimed at obtaining support for such a venture.

168

    (b) Schedule intermediate-level information sessions aimed at acceptance from some departments and tolerance from all in case of overlapping effects.

2. *Working with supervisory "families"—strictly departmental*

    (a) Provide two days of training, as discussed in the preceding chapter.

    (b) Allow two hours per week for at least four weeks, during which time the group continues work upon its items.

    (c) Assume that four or five weeks after the greenlight session the first items will be ready for implementation.

    (d) Administer the "Reaction to Your Job" questionnaire (if it is to be used at all) before the first item is implemented. Say as little as possible as to why it is being administered.

    (e) Agree upon the starting schedule and the order of introduction of new items.

    (f) Expect to spend six months to a year in the implementation stage.

    (g) Measure from month to month as usual; make a special effort to find new, relevant indicators which can be fed directly to an employee and which cover only his performance.

    (h) Readminister the "Reaction to Your Job" questionnaire only when the project is to be ended, as it cannot be readministered effectively very often.

With this two-phase, ten-step schedule covering six months' to a year's activity, one must conclude that a job improvement program is not merely a training course and certainly not merely a personnel gimmick. When turnover in a Saginaw, Michigan, division dropped from 29 percent to 23 percent and then on down to 21 percent, someone remarked skeptically to the division head that the results might be due entirely to a gimmick or the Hawthorne effect. His reply: "Well, if it is, I'm buying!"

By the end of a year, the job improvement approach to problems should be a way of life, proceeding informally whenever job changes arise—and arise they will. But it must be recognized that there will be no happy ending if someone does not watch the program carefully during its first year.

How to Organize for Work Itself

The question properly arises, therefore, "Who's in charge here?" The first-line supervisor is, absolutely, if a craft job is involved. (If the supervisor's job is being reshaped, the second level is in charge, and so on.) But the first-line supervisor will need help—not a lot, but some—for about a year. This help will come primarily from his boss, but the department's manpower utilization representative will also be of assistance.

In a big organization with many jobs and many people, there must be someone (let's call him the manpower utilization representative here) with these explicit responsibilities:

- To run the original work-itself workshop for a family group.
- To follow up every few weeks as the group refines its list of items and establishes priorities.
- To discuss problems that arise as a result of implementation (there will be some).
- To contact other groups or even other departments if they are affected by changes in practices, training, measurement procedures, and so on.
- To serve as consultant to individual members of families who want to greenlight informally about *other* jobs under their supervision. (Only one job need be formally greenlighted by a family.)
- To serve as consultant in the shaping of new jobs as they arise.
- To see that all management training courses contain materials that are compatible with these new concepts.

If departments are small, conceivably a manpower utilization person can service them and also act as the expert in this field for the total organization. Just as a modern corporation has the employment function and the training and development function, so it needs the manpower utilization function.

In reply to the question, "Who's in charge of a work-itself program or project?" we say:

1. The supervisor has absolute control.
2. A manpower utilization manager assigned by the department as a helper for the supervisor does not help run the unit, of course, but he helps the supervisor decide whether his proposed motivational moves are consistent and conceptually correct. This has paid off handsomely in the Treasury case (see Chapter 2).
3. More remotely, the specialist in the Personnel Department provides help. His job is to bring new departments along, to cross-fertilize, to watch turnover rates for signs of deteriorating job situations, to train interviewers and arrange for exit interviewing, and to work with task forces or others responsible for setting up new jobs. He is the staff man, pure but not simple—a specialist in a new area of knowledge.

REFINING THE ITEMS FURTHER

Two hours per week can be spent profitably in exploring more deeply the greenlight items, as they were left at the end of the second day. The conference leader should ask someone in the supervisory family to have the list typed from the easel sheets, preferably after they have been arranged in categories. He should not do this work for them; if they do not want their list, he surely does not.

Next, he should ask the supervisors to meet again, preferably without him. He might raise questions such as these for their second meeting, offering them individual copies of the list of questions as a memo:

1. What would be a good item to start with? Is there an item that *must* come first? In the Cross-Connection trial, the Keypunch trial, the Telephone Installers trial, the Engineering trial, and several others, the *first* item was the module of work.
2. Is there an item or two that employees will welcome? Can these be considered for use as starting privileges, thus win-

ning employee support for later items? (Remember, these are work privileges and responsibilities; they are *extensions* of the original job, not maintenance or bargained-for items, all of which should be treated separately from this project or program.)

3. Which half-dozen items appeal most to you as clear-cut ways for involving your employees personally in their work? Who will gain what?

4. How would we go about implementing the items you select? *Precisely* what will be said? What points will be presented in what order?

The first weekly meeting is devoted to further study of problems and obstacles and to a trial attempt to get a consensus on a starting point. A good opening item should maximize a chance for employee involvement while avoiding the risk of having the employees say, "More of the same old stuff; just another way to get more work out of us." It cannot be said too often that a work-itself project may improve performance, but this is not the reason behind the project.

The supervisors will unquestionably come up with items—or variations of items—that did not appear on the original greenlight list. Indeed, the conference leader should encourage them to listen to their employees for new ideas. (This last statement should come as a relief to those who believe job participation in which the employees can be the source of the original items is the best way. However, there is no point to employee participation if the supervisors are not ready. And getting them ready takes time.) The items will grow in specificity and detail as the four or five weekly meetings take place. By the fourth meeting, the sequence for introducing the new items (or responsibilities, privileges, changes, and motivators) will probably clear up.

By devoting time weekly to the job improvement program, a way of life is set up. "And where do we find the time?" someone may ask. Interestingly, the supervisory families do not complain about this. They say personnel matters always take time anyhow, every week; this is simply a refreshingly new approach. Many go so far as to make comments such as this: "At last I'm finding time to be a supervisor now that I've given up my role as chief clerk around here."

Help from Exit Interviews

Well-done interviews of people leaving the business can stimulate work-itself follow-up sessions, especially if they have been tape-recorded with the employee's permission. One such recording was played to a top executive. In it an operator talked about the damaging effects of using required set phrases in talking to customers. After listening to the entire recording, the executive shook his head and said, "I'm sorry; I didn't understand how the girls felt. That settles it; I'm willing to knock out the use of set phrases as an early greenlight item, if the rest of you want to." The problem is how to get tape recordings with this degree of authenticity.

Sad to say, most exit interviews are made by untrained interviewers who are not likely to be effective in cutting through the "cultural noise" of an exit interview. Employees who are leaving, especially if they go of their own volition, will always give "polite" reasons for quitting such as health, family, money, transportation. Paul Patinka of Western Electric Company provided this most helpful introductory statement for the exit interviewer: "Let your mind turn back, if you will. Tell me when you first started to think about leaving the company." This statement should be followed by what can be called first-level or factual probing of this kind: What happened to start you thinking along that line? What else might have started you off? Were there any other factors involved?

Then the interview should shift to the second level, or value probe: *Why* did this make you want to quit? (See the answer to Question 12, Chapter 6, also.)

As the interviewer grows in skill, he shifts back and forth from factual matters to values or beliefs until he understands why the employee is quitting. Interviews with nonmanagement employees often run from 30 minutes to a full hour. Those with managers are frequently longer than that. Repetitive or useless material can be deleted prior to the follow-up sessions by running the tape on one machine to a desirable section and then using a patch cord or some such device to transfer the words onto a blank on another machine. This edited tape will be much shorter; in fact, it may be made entirely of provocative excerpts from several exit interviews.

An actual tape provides the basis for helping the interviewer learn whether his interruptions, interpolations, or phrasing of questions is making an objective report on the job situation impossible. A wise beginner will try to get an experienced, trained interviewer (such as a college recruiter) to coach him.

Another advantage of a tape recording is that listeners can discern a trend over a period of one to ten months. If the very same questions elicit much more favorable responses over a period of time, it is fair to assume that the work-itself program is at least partly successful. For example, if "dissatisfaction with work" is displaced as a leading explanation by such reasons as "moving to another city," "pregnant," "illness in the family," then the trend is favorable; these reasons are beyond the control of the company. If this use of tape is projected, a definite set of questions and probes should be used in each interview with the first- and second-level probe questions as the core.

To interview all exiting employees may be an overwhelmingly large assignment at first. Consider, in that case, such steps as these to reduce the load:

1. Interview only those who are resigning or who have been dismissed. (Omit those going on leave, retiring, or transferring within the corporation and perhaps those others whose reason for leaving is not in question.)
2. Cover only a set percentage (every fourth person, for example) on some jobs.
3. Cover all persons in certain key jobs where turnover appears to be high or where other symptoms of work dissatisfaction are noted.
4. Don't bother to interview people from organizations where the boss is unconcerned about turnover. Where the boss *is* concerned, be his adjunct, his resource person.

There are two audiences for the tapes. First, every effort should be made to put together tapes that can help the supervisor who was in charge at the time of a resignation. Second, tapes should be heard by persons other than the immediate supervisor who may also be responsible for the situation, such as the men who set up the job, the equipment, the training, the measurement plan, or the rules.

How to Implement Items

There are three principal approaches to passing the final green-light items along to the employees:

1. Broadside—All employees in the group get the privilege, the responsibility, the feedback, and so on.
2. Deskside—Only those employees who clearly are reasonably well trained, responsible, dependable, and eager, and who have demonstrated ability are given the item. This is usually done in a conference at the supervisor's desk or at a man's work station. In any case it is done privately, not in a group.
3. Silent—Changes are made without notifying anyone.

The original Treasury study as conceived by the study directors was principally a *broadside* approach. But experience shows that supervisors prefer to work with their employees individually—that is, at *deskside*. The principle is clear: Bring every employee along just as fast as possible. Give responsibility whenever possible, and encourage an employee to accept it.

If he takes a responsibility and fails (makes an error), the supervisor *does not withdraw* the privilege or responsibility, nor does he start doing the employee's work for him. ("From now on, Joe, I'll look these over and sign them.") When there is an error, the supervisor helps the employee correct it, if need be, and then figure out what and why it happened. Supervisors prefer to do this "coaching" on an individual basis. All this is a long way from the group motivation approach.

How often should employees be given a new item? Some items can be given best in a bundle, a nest—especially if a significant change occurs in the module. For example, an engineer who is given all the step-by-step work for a particular group of central offices may need some related authorities at the same time. Or a new driver who finally gets his own truck can take over many aspects of responsibility for its maintenance all at once—its loading, deciding where it is to be parked, its security, and so on.

In general the introduction of items should be spread over a period of weeks or months, giving employees new responsibilities as they are able to assume them. But the program should be kept moving along.

The *silent* item, a concept that is a latecomer to work-itself projects, was conceived by supervisors in a number of places *after* the projects began. A silent item is a privilege or responsibility earned by an employee about which nothing is said. Here are two examples from one department:

1. After a tour changes at a switchboard and some operators have gone home, a remaining operator who moves from one position (location) to a vacant one for reasons of her own (light, heat, ventilation, or even whim) is not corrected or "reminded" provided she does it without ignoring the signal lights and thus inconveniencing customers.
2. An operator who talks to another, marks her toll cards in an unorthodox manner, or keys her toll calls in an unusual way is not corrected *if she does a good job* and does not interfere with other employees.

The "Golden Triangle" for Control of Implementation

In a number of the early studies, supervisors independently came up with a record sheet that is worthy of consideration at the implementation stage. The prospective items of change are identified at the heads of columns at the right and the names of the employees to be reached, either one at a time or broadside, are listed in a row at the left. At the points where row and column intersect, either a check mark or the date of implementation can be inserted for that employee.

A puzzling triangular pattern emerged in the early records. In abstract, it looked like this, with a check mark indicating the privilege was granted:

Employee	Item or Privilege from Greenlight Session						
	1	2	3	4	5	6	7
Sam	✓	✓	✓		✓		✓
Oscar	✓	✓		✓	✓	✓	✓
Bill	✓	✓	✓	✓	✓		
Terry	✓	✓		✓			
Jim	✓	✓	✓				
Joe	✓	✓					
James	✓						

When someone asked why James gets only *one* item, perhaps only a broadside one, the answer was, "Because he has been with us only one week!" On the other hand, Sam and Oscar may be experienced, dependable men who are under consideration for the next foreman's opening. Therefore, if a list is kept by seniority, it should not be surprising to see long strings of arrows extending across the top, since this is an elastic approach, not a geometrically rigid one.

The triangle breaks up any time the supervisor puts in a broadside item or lists names alphabetically. Such a chart is excellent both as a control instrument and as a progress report for the supervisor.

Taking Care of the Needs of Different Employees

This triangular concept of job improvement has other interesting consequences:

1. A job is not viewed as a little square, rigid box but as a loose triangle with many items still to be added at the right edge as the job changes. This flexible approach is important because a job shape fits an individual only at a certain point in time. He may later have more responsibility, and the triangular chart will show this.
2. If a job has very few items across the top, it probably is not basically a very rich job. Consider collapsing other functions with it, as described earlier.
3. The top persons in the triangle might be considered first

for promotion—provided, of course, that they have the other necessary qualifications. This dynamic way of appraising on-the-present-job performance shows which workers can take increased responsibility. The results of the Treasury trial were most impressive in this regard. Whether a person was likely to be a good supervisor became more obvious than it would have under some other appraisal system. Ability to take responsibility, to grow with a job, became the key.

4. If the top person is ill, is unable or unwilling to be a supervisor, or lacks interpersonal skills, obviously he should be passed over.

5. It bears repeating that people should not be treated as though they are all alike. This triangular approach truly permits differentiation according to ability or attitude. A job which gives all employees the same privileges and which has the same rectangular boundaries for all is the one in violation of the concept of human differences.

6. When an employee has few check marks despite the passage of adequate time, either reassignment to a different job or dismissal is suggested. Job improvement is anything but a soft approach to handling employees who cannot progress toward assuming the job responsibilities outlined across the top of the golden triangle for the job. The definiteness also gives an employee objective information about his job failure, since the chart is not run on a personality basis; the items steer clear of such criteria as "bad attitude," "uncooperative," "appearance," "tardy and absent." These are more likely to be the outputs or results of inability to perform well than the causes of it. The chart shows only what a man has or has not been given to do. It can be a good basis for discussion.

7. The triangular chart is frequently referred to as the continuation training chart. If the job module has been changed in the project or program, additional training may be called for. The triangular chart goes beyond mere training and asks, "Has he earned the right and does he want to take on the personal responsibility for production, quality, self-control, or whatever?"

8. There is nothing about the concepts of broadside, deskside, or silent items on the triangular control chart that hints at abandoning the job to the employees. Instead, the effort is

to turn over specific items of job performance to them while supervisors go on to their own tasks. (See Question 14 in Chapter 6.)

9. An occasional horizontal loader or maintenance item in the triangular chart should not cause alarm. Some "gray" items get in because of honest doubt, especially items involving status. (Placing one's name on the truck door is an example that was used earlier.) They will do no harm to a work-itself project or program, but they should not mislead us into thinking we have done big things for the work itself.

10. A work-itself program is an elastic, dynamic concept, running quite counter to more static job description and job evaluation concepts and those plans for salary administration which are based exclusively on term of service.

WHEN WILL GAINS APPEAR?

A major lesson from the follow up studies as compared to the original Treasury case is that such striking gains in six months are unusual. Directors of the other studies generally waited eight or ten months before readministering the "Reaction to Your Job" questionnaire; some waited a year. In the meantime, they watched the more easily measured results, such as production or turnover.

In retrospect, it seems that the rather quick gains in Treasury (six months) were the results of the interactions among such favorable factors as these:

1. A large proportion of well-educated women.
2. Few old-timers with rigid attitudes.
3. Excellent ability and cooperation on the part of supervisors.
4. Lack of delays that often occur when other departments are involved in decisions.
5. A relatively small group (28 girls) as compared to the very large Traffic Department trials (200 or more employees).
6. A job that was ripe for improvement.

Nevertheless, there will be signs of change—for the better in almost every case—as soon as a few items are installed. Some will be anecdotal in nature—little statements from employees who are beginning to sense that changes for the better are occurring. The voluntary report by the plant station installer (Chapter 7) was written only three weeks after he received his own area, truck, and so on. If the changes are being introduced deskside, results will obviously appear more slowly than they would with a broadside approach.

There is no need to be defensive about the slowness with which jobs are reshaped. Some of these jobs had been deteriorating slowly for many years. It is unreasonable to expect them to be repaired in a month or two. Most impatience for results comes not from the supervisors involved, but from the project or program director or from the newly appointed manpower utilization manager, whose eagerness is understandable.

TRAINING WILL BE AFFECTED

Obviously, job training can change quite radically if the job itself is changed through greenlight items. Those responsible for training must be brought into the project early; they might well be visitors at a work-itself workshop.

A major shift that should be considered by the trainers is *shortening* the training period. Can the new employee do more things on his own at an earlier date? Before the Treasury trial, for example, training had lasted eight weeks. By the end of the trial, however, correspondents were kept in a classroom situation only five weeks and, more important, wrote their first letters to shareholders over their own signatures on the third day of basic training. During the first four days, the correspondent also became accustomed to telephoning shareholders who had written letters that lacked essential information. The new correspondents were limited to simple problems, but they were wholly responsible for them.

This shift quickly takes mystery and fear of the unknown out of the job. There is solid evidence to show that training can be too long, too complex, and too discouraging as well as too short. As far as possible, the new training was oriented toward actual shareholder contacts rather than the usual classroom models and examples. Though the content did not necessarily change, the pace and identification of the correspondent with her job changed greatly.

As a result of this personal composition of replies in the first week, the trainers discovered another gain was possible. They could see by the end of two or three weeks when a given girl was not really suited for this task. Since there was no great training or emotional investment as yet, the trainers then tried to switch this girl into an assignment where she could indeed achieve, get recognition, and grow.

Suppose switching to a more suitable assignment was not a possible solution? Then the girl was dropped from the payroll, an act which was quick and final. This combination of training and accomplishment of some real work in the first week is both realistic and honest.

The improved likelihood of success is evident when we recall that the supervisor herself now has more time to train, since she does not have to verify and control each act of the experienced employee. The golden triangle concept for controlling both continuation training and the pressing of responsibility into employees' hands acts to guide and remind the supervisor-coach.

Not too much experience except the Treasury example is at hand. However, precisely the same principles that provide job satisfaction to experienced employees should be used in the early days of training. The sooner an employee can perform a responsible piece of work, the better. Advanced training can continue concurrently with actual work accomplishment.

MEASURING RESULTS AND KEEPING THE RECORD

If the Treasury case is convincing, it is largely because the records that were kept support the findings. Whether a project or a program is undertaken, someone is sure to ask, "Is it a success?" The decision as to which measures should be kept should be formal and not left to happenstance. In every project, time is allotted on the second day to a discussion of what measures will show whether the effort is successful. Even in the case of a program, the same question should be considered, if only briefly. The following remarks apply especially to projects.

In some trials, notably Engineering, the measures had to be tailor-made. In a true sense, every employee has a "customer," someone who wants his work and receives it. In Engineering, questionnaires were evolved to be sent to the customers of the engineers, the people who order additions to the equipment in an existing central office or a whole new office. The measurement plan called for sending questionnaires to these customers at the start of the study and again at its conclusion. The engineers have another important contact, the manufacturer of the equipment, who was quizzed as to the quality of the specifications before and after the study period.

The point is this: In most businesses, proof must be objective if it is to be accepted. Next, ingenuity may be required in order to come up with meaningful measures. Also, the before-and-after approach is a wise one if a project is to determine whether the organization is doing better than it had been.

Still another point on measurement should be considered—using similar measures on a control group. The need for this measure should become obvious from this actual example from one of the trials:

| | Customer Service Index 1966 | | | |
	June	July	August	September
Achieving group	72	66	72	74
Control group	73	55	44	38

Had achieving group results alone been available, the verdict would have been "no progress" although the gain was actually substantial. To stay level was an accomplishment in the face of the general decline revealed by the control data.

Why not simply compare this year's performance with last year's? If this were done, last year's data would be the control or comparison data for this year's performance. Quite clearly, this would have been erroneous in the case just cited, because the results for the achieving group (not shown) were approximately equal for both years. Only data from an outside control group revealed the drop. Perhaps it should be noted that the managers of both groups and top management feel they can interpret the data in the light of what they know to have been happening in the company and in the economy. Fortunately, the control data saved the day.

Good measurement and good accounting procedures demand that the costs of this program be considered. There may be large operating gains. But they were not without cost. What were their costs? One thinks of the cost of the original two-day meeting and the out-of-pocket expenses for any follow-up ones. Were extra trucks bought? If any other capital costs arose, what were they? Did any change in operating practices cost money? Was it a one-time change, or does it continue? Fair reporting demands that the costs of the manpower utilization effort be stated. And, as was done in Chapter 2, the offsetting gains can be shown.

Finally, who will keep the record? Once the measures are agreed upon, someone has to be put in charge of gathering the information on them and writing the report. He should also collect anecdotal and illustrative materials; to know that trend lines move up or down is not to know why. In the Bell System studies, this job goes to the project director. Part of his effort is to find out what's going on in the control groups without injecting work-itself ideas in any way. Whether their results improve or not, he should be prepared to give the views of the control group managers as to the cause.

Just how rigorous the proof shall be should be decided on the second day of the workshop or prior to the day when the first items of change are introduced. After that, it will be too late. Perhaps other measures can be reconstructed later, but not all the important ones.

In short if work itself is undertaken with full belief in its efficacy, no special data or records are required. But if proof is needed, these two decisions should be reached formally: (1) What data are needed? (2) Who shall be the keeper and reporter of the data?

REINFORCING EARLY EFFORTS

The department (or Personnel Department) manpower utilization man must sensitively steer between too much aid and not enough. If his contacts with the third-level boss indicate that the first-level supervisors are refining their list and are holding meetings on some reasonable schedule, he should not ask to be part of the effort. He might suggest that he and the third- or fourth-level bosses go over the supervisors' tentative plan before implementation starts. The knowledge that such a step is being considered will act to keep the family working. Four or five weeks should be the maximum time away from the group.

The accounting procedure for the disposition of the items should be fairly formal. "Just what has been done since I saw you last?" His job is to provide a mirror for their efforts and their plans; he should have none of his own. He is the consultant now, reinforcing their efforts if they are on the beam. Only if they are off the beam does he help them.

These contacts will continue for months. The manpower consultant must not abandon the family at any time. As some new consultant-to-group inputs that can be helpful from time to time, consider:

- Sending out stimulating articles on the work-itself theme.
- Projecting a new (to them) film on motivation, such as one of those directed by Saul Gellerman in the Bureau of National Affairs series.
- Playing a tape recording of a stimulating interview (exit or on-the-job) with an employee.
- Having a speaker from a project or program that operated successfully.

During the first six months or even during the entire year of the project or program, the introduction of *new* theories or competing ideas on motivation may actually interfere unless the job is done thoughtfully, *but*, for the long run, the notion of introducing other points of view is a good one. A well-trained supervisor ought to be able to cope with new theories without being knocked off his course. Toward the end of the first year, the expectation is high that the supervisor will have seen enough results so that the work-itself approach to motivating employees will not need outside reinforcement.

An Overview of the
Work-Itself Idea

THIS CLOSING CHAPTER CONSISTS SOLELY OF THE AUTHOR'S IDEAS and opinions, not those of the Bell System, although the corporation does not necessarily disagree with the basic position set forth here. The statement of the problem, the strategy employed to meet it, and the results are scarcely open to question. But the final sections of the chapter are interpretations of data and one man's point of view about the nature of work.

THE PROBLEM OF JOBS

The problem that precipitated these studies is employee dissatisfaction with work, which is evidenced in steadily mounting turnover rates. That this problem is widespread was shown by the many inquiries about these studies from other businesses.

Careful exit interviewing brought out the usual wide range of reasons for quitting--inadequate pay, undesirable hours, bad transportation, home problems, poor supervision, and undesirable work. The Bell System has worked reasonably hard to correct these problems or, when they cannot be corrected, to alleviate them. Take night work, for example. Night tours of duty for some employees are facts we have to live with in any business that operates around the clock every day, without time off even for Christmas. This is a limiting factor in any effort to decrease dissatisfaction. Does this limiting condition apply to the *jobs* we do, also? Must they, like the tours of duty, be what they are? Are they causing trouble unnecessarily?

Strategy for Improving Jobs

The work of Professor Herzberg and others suggested strongly that the work itself was a powerful motivator of employees under certain conditions. The Herzberg survey study of 200 management men probed the causes of job satisfaction and dissatisfaction. AT&T's experimental studies started where the Herzberg study left off; they involved several thousand employees in achieving groups spread across nine different nonsupervisory jobs in ten associated companies of the Bell System.

In all cases the work itself—the task—was the variable in the experimental groups and was held as constant as possible in the control groups. In both experimental and control groups the factors that surround the work itself—variously labeled maintenance or hygiene items—were also held constant.

In each of the experimental trials, a family of immediate supervisors tried to solve this problem: How can we shape a particular job so that the job incumbent has, not more work, but more responsibility for the work? How can we make him feel that a part of the business is his alone, that he can make decisions regarding it and personally identify with it? If we can do this, the employee will have a heightened chance for individual achievement and for recognition of his achievement. In addition, he will have a chance to learn and to grow on his job, perhaps to be promoted. Furthermore, if we can do this, we can make the employee's working life a more meaningful human experience. If we succeed, he will not feel impelled to look elsewhere for good work or to become so unproductive as to be useless to the company.

Here are two illustrations of how employees are given responsibility. In the first, a service representative usually decides when a customer's service should be cut off for failure to pay a bill. She reported her decision to her supervisor, who checked the facts and the reasoning and usually obtained the signature of someone still higher in management. Then service was discontinued until the customer paid his bill. In the work-itself program, after the representative has repeatedly demonstrated her good judgment, she orders the cutoff directly. If the customer pays the overdue bill, the representative involved can really feel that *she* was successful. And if she has made an error in judgment, it is her error, not the supervisor's. Thus responsibility, a major motivator, is increased for the employee.

The second illustration comes from a large foreign chemical company where six studies similar to those reported in this book are in progress. Although the sales volume in dollars is high for a certain line of chemicals, the profit margin is dropping. The salesmen have been doing an excellent job of selling chemicals that have low margins and competitively favorable prices but they have not done well at selling lines with better profit margins. However, the salesmen were not aware of this.

In this project, the experimental group was given pricing information, including the lower and upper bounds that have to be observed in setting the price of any chemical. Next, they were acquainted with the profitability problem and were asked, in effect, to "act for the company. Set the price at the level that you think will result in a sale and help to overcome the profitability slide." After six months of applying this technique the experimental group is reported to be running almost three-quarters of a million dollars ahead of the control group in profitability of sales. The control group, in contrast, is still merely following the book in setting prices. In the service representative illustration and in this one, the challenge is to find ways, big or little, whereby an employee can earn the right to act for the company.

As these sessions with families of supervisors proceeded (never cross-sectional or interdepartmental groups), the technique of greenlighting was developed whereby highly specific items or ideas were produced to make a job more meaningful and more interesting. For competent people with demonstrated ability, jobs can be improved by steps such as these:

1. Give the employee a good module of work.
   - Pull responsibilities back down to this job level if they have been assigned higher up only for safety's sake.
   - Gather together the responsibilities that are now handled by people whose work precedes or follows, including verifying and checking.
   - Push certain routine matters down to lower-rated jobs.
   - Automate the routine matter completely if possible.
   - Rearrange the parts and divide the total volume of work, so that an employee has a feeling of "my customers," "my responsibility."
2. Once an employee has earned the right, let him really run his job.
3. Develop ways for giving employees *direct*, individual feedback on their own performance (not group indexes).
4. Invent ways of letting the job expand so that an employee can grow psychologically. ("There's always something new coming up on this job!")

Such steps as these four principles of job improvement should result in better jobs for employees. Since employees want meaningful work, they should like the improved job better, and turnover should drop in locations where it once was high. In other jobs that are handled by older people who don't quit but who do give other evidences of job dissatisfaction (low productivity, grievances, and so on) improvement should be attainable simply by concentrating on the question: How can we make this as good a task or assignment as possible and practical?

SOME SURPRISINGLY GOOD RESULTS

Of the nineteen studies nine were rated "outstandingly successful," one was a complete "flop," and the remaining nine were "moderately successful." The most striking single piece of evidence was a 13 percent drop in the turnover rate among a large sample of service representatives at a time when the control group rate increased by 9 percent. Other technical results (productivity, quality of performance, customer reaction, and so on) either improved slightly or at least held their own. If the turnover rate across the Bell

System could be dropped by only 10 percentage points (to use a conservative figure) the savings in training costs on this one job alone would be in millions of dollars.

The biggest error one could make in interpreting the data would be to contend that these good results came from increased skill at "keeping people busy." In the first place, a typical service representative is never "unbusy." She is always very busy indeed. But supervisors in the test locations found ways of letting trained service representatives be *more* responsible for their customers in a meaningful way than they had ever been before. As a result, the desire to quit apparently dropped and other indicators improved slowly.

While permanence of the gains is still to be established for 18 of the 19 studies, the original Treasury Department results show *excellent* long-range promise. After three years, the Treasury correspondents' service index for all units (achieving and control alike) is now in the upper 90's.

No claim is made that these 19 trials cover a representative sample of jobs and people within the Bell System. For example, there were no trials among the manufacturing or laboratory employees, nor were all operating companies involved. There are more than a thousand different jobs in the Bell System, not just the nine in these studies. What to make of the results, then?

Even this limited sample of the universe of jobs shows that significant changes can be made in some jobs and that striking improvements will result. In other cases, not much will happen, although no losses will occur in the effort to improve jobs. These are the most likely probabilities if we take more samples of the same jobs, but there is no way of predicting whether good results will occur with a new job.

THE FUTURE OF THE EFFORT

What will be done with the findings in the companies that conducted the studies? The reaction throughout the Bell System has generally been, "We don't see how we can afford not to go ahead." There is to be no crash program; we made it clear that these results usually required eight months to a year of patient, persistent work. In general, any department in any location, systemwide, may go ahead *with the active support and concurrence of headquarters.* Men in all departments at headquarters have been made available to help start either projects or programs in the field.

For the most part, however, the project stage is past. Most departments, both at headquarters and in the field, now ask to start *programs*. This implies that no data will be collected from a control group; that is, no group will be asked to "hold still" for a year. Therefore, evalution will generally be in terms of a group's own past performance.

A small manpower utilization group with these explicit responsibilities has been set up at AT&T headquarters.

1. Spread current knowledge and techniques.
2. Act as consultants on current job structures.
3. Continue to probe for new understanding of the reasons jobs go wrong; get the principles refined.
4. Serve as consultants to field people who are setting up new jobs, a never-ending process in such an expanding industry as communications.

Quite clearly AT&T is settling down for the long haul. Seventy-seven new programs have been started. No one expects all jobs to be equally improvable, nor is every job in need of assistance. And, since there are so many requests, the accepted view is, "Don't push any manager who is uncertain or lukewarm in his interest. Reach him later."

At this writing, more than 50 companies outside the Bell System have requested further information about the studies. Some were already conducting their own studies; others have now started here in the United States and abroad. A reasonably safe prediction is that much more information will be available within the next ten years as to how one bridges the gap from theory to fact. Experimental studies, not surveys, will probably make the difference as knowledge in this field accumulates (see the answer to Questions 16 and 20, Chapter 6).

Some Truths About Work

One reason not all managers rush into this program is that it means extensive change and not trivial change at that. Placing his photograph above each employee's work position won't suffice, but it is a project that could be set up in one "crash" week. Making basic changes in a well-established job is hard work, mentally and emotionally. After working on improving the jobs of the people they supervise, managers have often been heard to say, "What am I doing to my own job!"

Many a supervisor rose to his present job by performing well on each job in turn on the way up. To have kept these jobs rather than to have become a turnover statistic himself might be viewed as a reflection on his own ability. But, in spite of the likelihood of emotional involvement when changing a familiar job, personal feelings do not get in the way very frequently either in workshop sessions or among the highly placed managers when proposals for change are brought to them. Even the man who may be responsible for the fix a job is in is usually glad to find a solution. Occasionally, a particular executive has struggled too hard to save an old job rather than accept the changes proposed by lower-level supervisors in the greenlight sessions, but this is the exception.

There are no villains, no evil people who deliberately deprive employees of job satisfaction. When past steps have resulted in inadvertent job denuding, these steps were usually taken to achieve other desirable ends.

Still another basic truth is uncovered when we ask, "Why have these projects gone well?" We let it be known that six new projects were needed in order to check out the original Treasury study. We got three times that number in a matter of weeks, even though the executive level had only the results of one study to judge by. And, since the new programs are doing very well indeed, many other managers want to start.

The basic truth here is that managers *want* employees to do well and to have good jobs. "After all," one said, "I work here too." John W. Gardner suggests that *there can be no institutional change without aspiration.*[1] The fact that managers reach toward the work-itself goal indicates that they do aspire to present their employees with rich job opportunities.

The aspiration of good jobs for all employees is matched by similar aspirations for the other two legs of the corporate stool. There is no doubt at all that a sensible corporation aspires to give better service to *customers* also. More than 15,000 employees in the

---

[1] John W. Gardner, *No Easy Victories*, Harper & Row, New York, p. 44.

Bell Telephone Laboratories, for example, are working essentially toward new and better services. And on the *shareholder's* side, in an era when his equity can erode because of rapid inflation, the corporation has given repeated evidence that it aspires to keep its shareholder financially above the tide of inflation.

There is a direct connection between job improvement projects and one of Gardner's statements:

> The release of human potential, the enhancement of individual dignity, the liberation of the human spirit—those are the deepest and truest goals to be conceived by the hearts and minds of the American people. And those are ideas that sustain and strengthen a great civilization—if we believe in them, if we are honest about them, if we have the courage and the stamina to live for them.[2]

What is the connection? The studies were founded on the premise that jobs could be improved—and then set out to do it by releasing human potential more completely. In Gardner's words:

> Of all the ways in which society serves the individual, few are more meaningful than to provide him with a decent job. . . . It isn't going to be a decent society for any of us until it is for all of us. If our sense of responsibility fails us, our sheer self-interest should come to the rescue.[3]

Some people may assume that Gardner was talking about the hard-core unemployed. Actually, he was talking about a just society for all; but in any case his words amply support the aphorism, "A difference which makes no difference is not different."

A statement of deep truth that appeared at the time of these studies was made by the Negro psychologist Kenneth B. Clark, who said:

> The roots of the multiple pathology in the dark ghetto are not easy to isolate. They do not lie primarily in unemployment. In fact, if all of its residents were employed it would not materially alter the pathology of the community. More relevant is the status

[2]*Ibid.* p. 16.
[3]*Ibid.*, p. 25.

of the jobs held . . . more important than merely having a job,
is the kind of job it is.[4]

Ultimately there is no truth for the black employee that is not
equally a truth for the white. To help a hard-core person get started
management may want to take a job apart for a while. It may at
first give him not the whole module or task—the installation and
repair of telephones, for example—but the recovery of telephone
handsets that were left in apartments, homes, or offices when tenants
moved. Then he can learn how to install a telephone and eventually
perform the more difficult task of figuring out why an instrument
refuses to work.

Nothing more will be said here about minority problems, differences between male and female employees, or college graduates
versus high school or grade school graduates simply because we
have not found (*in these studies*) that the differences make a difference. Even the question of how to improve jobs for older employees
as distinct from younger ones has not proved to be a critically
important problem. *The major problem* is how to improve the job
for any human being. That's why work itself, not the manipulation
of people, has been repeatedly presented as the crucial variable.

And Gardner is quite right when he says, "our sheer self-interest
should come to the rescue." This is one employee program that can
be cost-free in as little as one year. In contrast, most employee
programs end up as added costs of doing business.

There are still some people who would debate these issues. One
spokesman explicitly said that these work-itself studies are misdirected. In his opinion, what employees need is "more close-order
drill, more discipline." He said that the lack of discipline in American
industry today is causing excessive turnover, grievances, and strikes.
Although he made no suggestion as to how to achieve this discipline,
one might observe that all it takes is military conscription (a kind of
compulsory employment office), prisons for poor performers and
objectors to the proposed employment, and, in some countries, a
wall against which to stage executions.

Still another view of work that needs to be dealt with holds that
the "work ethic" or "Protestant ethic" idea is outdated. By 1985,

[4]Kenneth B. Clark, "Explosion in the Ghetto," *Psychology Today*, September
1967.

Americans will be able to live at the level of their present standard of living by working only six months a year. Or, alternatively, if a man chooses to work year-round, he will be able to retire from work at age 38.[5] Enough rise in the gross national product is expected to make this feasible. People must get ready for handling leisure, and the unmistakable implication of the report is that the work ethic has prepared us poorly for such a life.

And so it has. The disputable point is not the accuracy of the prediction; it is the implication that work is not or cannot be as enjoyable as is a hobby or a sport such as golf or fishing. Gardner states the case for the potential satisfactions of work:

> What could be more satisfying than to be engaged in work in which every capacity or talent one may have is needed, every lesson one may have learned is used, every value one cares about is furthered?
>
> No wonder men and women who find themselves in that situation commonly overwork, pass up vacations, and neglect the less exciting games such as golf.
>
> It is one of the amusing errors of human judgment that the world habitually feels sorry for overworked men and women— and doesn't feel a bit sorry for the men and women who live moving from one pleasure resort to the next. As a result, the hard workers get not only all the real fun but all the sympathy too, while the resort habitués scratch the dry soil of calculated diversion and get roundly criticized for it. It isn't fair.[6]

What seems likely is that people of the future will learn to struggle against jobs that are unnecessarily bad. The willingness of management in many companies to improve the work itself should give courage to those who believe men should not write off the work portion of their lives while getting ready for the new leisure. Obviously one portion yields money, the other does not. But the point is this: Both the work *and* the leisure portions should be and can be challenging and interesting. The right mix will vary from person to person.

[5]*The New York Times*, April 7, 1968, report of a new study conducted by Southern California Research Council.

[6]Gardner, *op. cit.*, p. 32.

How Long Will It Last?

The concept of work just outlined grew out of the studies, as have the views as to how long a person will find his job improved, a question that arises repeatedly. In the first place, not all jobs have equal potential for yielding satisfaction. Some will be fairly routine even when we have reshaped them as best we can. In this case, the goal is still to give the employee all the responsibility possible in running the job.

A woman in one of our studies volunteered to take on a routine clerical assignment that recurred four times a year, a job that involved replacing lost, mislaid, or mutilated checks—the sort of job that automation can never eliminate. When asked why she volunteered for a second time to perform this "dum-dum" job, she replied, "Well, it may be a dum-dum job, but at least it's *my* dum-dum job the way we now run it." An important implication of these studies is that routine work, especially if everyone recognizes that it must be done, can be made more acceptable if we maximize the personal responsibility component. Although this may not be the world's greatest job, employees will find it worthwhile if they are allowed to run it in a self-responsible way.

The substantial reduction in turnover indicates that we can slow down the onset of dissatisfaction. Part of the long-range job of a supervisory family is to plan a *series* of steps so that an employee can feel he is still learning, still growing. He should be able to advance within his current job, as well as upward to the next job level. Unless a job has very elastic boundaries and psychological growth and learning can occur, it will eventually bore its incumbents. People, like plants, may need to be repotted occasionally, at least until the pot is big enough for the specimen to grow without stunting. Once we have done our best to make a good and challenging job, the onset of boredom will vary with the ability of the incumbents. For some, the job may be good for a lifetime; for others, only a few years. If we have been reasonably good at selection, placement, and training, as well as job shaping, no one will be bored in only a few weeks or months.

The whimsical "Peter Principle" holds that men rise in a business hierarchy until they reach their own level of incompetence. There they stay, since they are incompetent to go ahead. If a battle of principles were to break out, we would present in opposition the Ford Principle, which is that "a man tends to repot himself until he finds a pot that is big enough." Not all people succeed in finding such a pot, of course. This puts men (or employees) into three classes.

> Class 1—Men in pots that are too big for them (as suggested by the Peter Principle).
> Class 2—Men in pots that are just right.
> Class 3—Men in pots too small for them.

Class 1 is no cause for worry; surely not too many men are in it. Those men in Class 2 are to be envied. It's Class 3 that is bothersome.

Applying the Ford Principle, we should not cut men down to fit the pots we need to fill; we should instead get bigger pots—enlarge the jobs—and let our men grow to fill them. To put it another way, if our round pegs (people) do not fit our square holes (jobs) ream the holes to the pegs; don't ram the pegs into the holes any which way or cut them down to fit. In other words, change the shape of the jobs and you improve the level of employee satisfaction; cut the employees down to fit the job and you perpetuate existing troubles and perhaps breed new ones.

WILL FUTURE STUDIES TURN OUT AS WELL?

Progress over the past two or three years has led us to conclude that the measured results, shown in Chapters 2 and 3, are an understatement of what can be achieved eventually. Some handicaps were built into the study designs for scientific reasons, such as the need to minimize the Hawthorne effect. Experience shows that if employees know that they are part of a special study or campaign, results drop off again when the campaign is over. Therefore, we never told the employees that studies were under way or that we were going to try to improve their jobs. We simply did it, at first not very expertly. In 16 of the 19 studies, we did not tell even the first-level supervisors that systematic approach to job improvement was under way simply to block their being either for or against the idea of improving motivation through the work itself.

In the future, either projects or programs *should* provide richer yields for these reasons:

1. First-level supervisors can be informed, along with upper levels. The complete family will have better greenlight ideas than the smaller supervisory family we used (second, third, and fourth levels). Acts inconsistent with the principles will occur less frequently once the immediate supervisor is both informed and included.
2. The topmost levels should be informed also so that inconsistent ideas, orders, and plans do not come down from above.
3. Sometimes good ideas for improving one job are blocked unless other jobs, even other departments, are involved. In the project stage, we had to forgo involving other jobs and departments; but they should be involved in future programs.
4. When supervisory people in *many* locations are working simultaneously to reshape a given job, cross-fertilization of ideas actually occurs. In only one study were we able to take advantage of this.
5. The training workshops (Chapter 7) have improved because of the early trials.
6. Only after the studies were well along did we discover the crucial importance of devising feedback schemes for individual employees (as opposed to group indexes).

Considering all these factors, future efforts should be more productive than the original trials, especially if they are programs available to any supervisory family, rather than limited to a trial or project group. This does not imply that a program will be *any easier* than the trials; good greenlight items will always be hard to come by. But results should be at least as striking, if not more so.

THE PRINCIPLES OF JOB ENRICHMENT

At the start of this series of studies, many tape recordings were made wherein employees talked about their jobs, especially upon quitting. Many remarks were heard repeatedly: "I'm tired of being treated like a child." "I didn't think this would be like school, but it is." "I don't want to be simply a 'hey-boy' for someone else." There is no indication that times will change, that people will once again come to employment offices begging for work, or that they will stay when they don't want to, as they have at times in the past. The roots of the disenchantment must be dealt with. Much of the disenchantment can be traced to the early 1900's, when industry went through a period of job engineering and stopwatch analyses of work flow. Then job designs, job specifications, job rules, job regulations, and highly detailed work practices were developed. In many interviews, employees specifically complain about being caged in by these rules.

In such a work situation, the supervisor's job may seem to be that of keeper of the caged-in people. And his major motivational task might be viewed as that of rattling the cages so that the drowsy animals "look alive." In this analogy motivation is from *outside:* the keeper does it. Many managers now believe that this approach to work motivation has had its day.

How to go forward, then? How to view employees? The data from these studies show that it is possible to get an order-of-magnitude change, not just a small increment. Modern employees are bright, healthy, well fed, and well educated compared to those in the time-and-motion study days. They will not accept dull jobs unless the jobs are their very own. We must set the conditions of work so as to gradually maximize the responsibility thrust upon the worker. To do this we must ask ourselves these questions:

- What do I do for him that he could now do for himself?
- What thinking can he now do for himself?
- What goals could we now set *jointly?*
- What advanced training or skill could he now have?
- What job could he work toward now? How could I help him?
- Is there a way of combining this job with another one that he would like? Is the module right?
- Is there anything he does that could be given to a lower-rated job?
- Can anything be automated out of the job?

The trouble, then, with a straight engineering approach to work flow, job layout, and job specifications is that employees won't stay on these jobs—as evidenced by turnover rates for highly rationalized, tightly structured jobs. We must learn to trade off engineering economies for human values and not to assume that this will be costly. Actually, every day beyond the old median length of tenure that a service representative, for example, stays on a newly reshaped job is of cash value to the business. We are quite sure that she *will* stay if she can get more satisfaction from her work.

Job satisfaction is hard to describe, hard to visualize. It will not make an employee go around with a big, happy grin on his face. More typical of his expression would be that of the golfer, the athlete, the chess player, trying to make a good shot or to perform well. The face and attitude of any well-motivated worker confronted by a difficult, challenging situation are more like those of the athlete than those of the relaxed watchers in the stands.

Job satisfaction may or may not be tied to happiness. But we will know that we are doing something right if we can change the conditions of the job so that employees will stay on and work productively. For the older workers, the test will be whether they are with us in spirit as well as in body. The way to achieve this end, for new or old employees, is not to confront them with demands, but to confront them with demanding, meaningful work. And the employee will always have the last word as to whether the work is meaningful.

Appendix A

Treasury Department Manpower Utilization

by Malcolm B. Gillette

Treasury Department Manpower Utilization

by Malcolm B. Gillette

THIS APPENDIX SUMMARIZES SOME OF THE WORK-ITSELF APPROACHES and methods and shares some of the experiences of the employees in the Treasury Department.

Almost all our efforts have been concentrated on helping the managers at each level to examine and apply work-itself concepts to the jobs for which they are immediately responsible. A deep understanding, a sincere acceptance and support of the program at all management levels are necessary before profitable application can begin. Individual managers have difficulty trying to do this job alone.

We have found that the work-itself concept is applicable to *all* levels because, once started, all persons and departments in the organization are affected. Both managerial and craft jobs *can* be enriched in meaningful ways, but strong support from line management is essential for successful implementation. Although it is still too soon to know all that might be accomplished under a program such as this, the managers are getting some significant results.

BACKGROUND OF THE EXPERIMENT

The original work-itself experiment was conducted between March and September 1965 in Shareowner Communications. Job enrichment concepts were applied to the jobs of 28 correspondents reporting to four first-line supervisors. Only the fourth-, third-, and second-level managers who supervised these people needed to understand what was being done. By contrast, the current effort requires that some 250 management people at all levels acquire real understanding of work motivation and its application to their own jobs and to the jobs of the 900 employees who report to them.

The main thrust of activity has been centered in the Stock and Bond Division, since this is where the great bulk of our people work. However, the Financial and Earnings Divisions have also participated in parts of the program.

Basic questions. The changeover from an experimental study to a broad work-itself program begins with questions. Just as the Treasury Department had to face and answer these questions, so will any organization that undertakes such a program. The questions range from "How do you know you need it? Will it help?" through "At what management level do you start?" How will upper management recognize and reward a manager who is an expert at utilizing the talents of his people?"

TRAINING EFFORT

Since it is the manager who will decide on and make whatever changes occur, he must know clearly what his responsibilities are in the area of the work itself. He must also become familiar enough with the work-itself concepts to make many judgments and decisions. He must be able to determine whether the work his people do is meaningful to them and to the organization, whether the changes he makes will be profitable over the long run, and whether they will reduce recruiting, training, and turnover costs. This demands an extensive training effort, one that depends upon and promotes self-motivation in development.

The on-the-job training program which makes this possible requires from 9 to 18 months and uses various combinations of group discussions, individual interviews with managers, reading material, and films. It is divided into three parts.

1. *Manpower utilization—the broad view.* This initial phase has a dual purpose: understanding and commitment. The managers explore the new concepts developed by the behavioral sciences and come to under-

stand what people are looking for in a job today—responsibility, recognition, achievement, opportunity, interesting work, and growth. With developing understanding each manager begins to recognize the need to use the human resources available more effectively and comes to the conviction that policies and practices must continually be reviewed and adjusted in order to do so. The three areas covered in this stage are:

a. Maintenance and motivation concepts as they relate to the work situation.
b. Influence of the manager on the development and growth of his subordinates.
c. Development, growth, and change.

2. *Implementation.* The manager's focus becomes more specific in this phase. Through his understanding of the factors that make jobs more meaningful to people, he recognizes the possible gains for the company as well as the individual. He then begins to actively apply this knowledge. He examines the content of those specific jobs for which he himself is responsible in order to determine what things are still needed, and he begins to seek ways to build them in, while at the same time creating a climate conducive to change. At this point he begins to concentrate on enriching each subordinate's job individually.

After he has a good grasp of the ideas and has begun to see ways of implementing them, he attends a three-day conference on "Managing for Growth." This conference is designed to continue the development of those skills which will assist the manager in forming his people into a more effective workforce. The three main topics are (1) how people learn, (2) trends of development toward maturity in an individual, and (3) learning and growth in a job situation. These topics are interwoven into a series of exercises utilizing the managers' on-the-job experiences and problems. The three days are really a continuation of the manager's job in an off-the-job atmosphere which affords him the opportunity to concentrate on ways to apply his recently acquired knowledge.

Those managers who have an ability and a desire to provide their people with meaningful jobs have been doing *just that* for years, so fuller utilization of employees' talents is not a new concept, *it's just good managing!* It is giving employees what they currently expect in a job—and they expect not only to be treated well but also to get the chance to show what they can do. Feedback from the managers who have attended these conferences indicates that they not only acquire new skills but begin to confront some basic questions about their role as managers.

3. *Evaluation of the program.* This part of the training effort in-

volves a continuous evaluation of the results of the program and of individual performance to ascertain the program's value to the company.

In the Stock and Bond Division, a comparison of the first 11 months of 1967 with the same months of 1966 points up some encouraging results. For example:

- Productivity and service indexes improved.
- Greater number of employees indicated job satisfaction.
- Nonsupervisory management force losses (excluding losses for reasons of retirement, maternity, and transfer to other Bell System assignments) decreased 27 percent (35 people), saving an estimated $245,000 in recruiting, training, and turnover costs.

EFFECTS ON RESULTS

When attention is focused on a job or unit, the interest and recognition are likely to produce increased effort and improved production and quality; the Hawthorne studies proved this. But, as the managers begin to assign more *real* responsibility to people whose work efforts have been watched closely and controlled in the past, some indexes dip until the employees comprehend the meaning of being held fully responsible and accountable for their work. Exhibit 3 in Chapter 2 on the communications service index for correspondent groups indicates the occurrence of this pattern in 1966.

OTHER BENEFITS

When a program like this gets under way with the velocity that it has in the Stock and Bond Division, it is difficult to distinguish between those changes and resultant savings that would have happened anyway and those changes that came about because of the managers' knowledge of job enrichment. A few of the things that the supervisors in the Stock and Bond Division have accomplished in an 18-month period are outlined in these pages. This has been a difficult period for them because the number of shareowners has increased, the volume of work has increased, programming work undertaken for the general departments has increased threefold, there has been a switch from one computer to another—and the managers have been in the throes of moving half the Division to New Jersey. Nevertheless, accomplishments have been substantial.

Shareowner communications. The investigation and file clerk jobs were reviewed according to the principles of the work-itself concept. Assignments were rearranged, and those jobs that could not be improved were automated by use of Xerox machines and lectrievers. The force was reduced from 46 to 24 clerks, and one second-level and two first-level jobs were eliminated at a total annual saving in salaries of $135,000.

The correspondents' work was also reviewed. The simpler and routine cases were turned over to the next lower level, loading both jobs and providing a source of future correspondents. With the correspondents taking on more of what used to be supervisory responsibilities, management has been able to reduce the number of second-level supervisory jobs from 4 to 3, first-level from 16 to 12, and work verifiers from 4 to 0, resulting in an annual salary saving of $76,000.

Stock and bond operations. In the stock transfer group some parts of the work formerly handled by the stock transfer assistants have been passed down the line to clerical levels and part-time employees, freeing the stock transfer assistants for the more complex work. At the same time this action reduces the need for additional people at that level. The total saving is approximately $40,000.

In addition, the managers in the stock transfer group and the methods group developed an arrangement which combined the employee stock-pension unit with the dividend reconciliation unit, resulting in an annual work and salary saving of about $100,000.

Data systems and processing. As programmers have been trained and developed, some tasks and job functions formerly handled by second- and third-level managers have been turned over to the programmers themselves. These specialists are now consulting with clients, writing entire programs, and combining these programs into systems. As a result, the third-level managers are now working as administrators in the conceptual area of planning and organizing.

Personnel, training, and results. In the personnel section college recruiters, who were previously second and third level, are now first-level people. The functions of the results supervisor, training supervisor, and personnel supervisor—all full third-level jobs—were rearranged and combined into one assignment.

As a result of the learning and experiences cited here, the Treasury organization has come to think of the work-itself theory as synonymous with fuller utilization of manpower *talent*. Implementation is the examination of each job by the immediate supervisor to determine whether that job assures the fullest possible utilization of the abilities of the person performing the job. This is important because, in an organization that is already functioning smoothly, this offers the greatest opportunities for positive effects on ultimate cost.

DIFFICULTIES AND COSTS

Difficulties. It is hard to avoid overmanaging, overdirecting, and making decisions that subordinates could make. If the quality or productivity declines, it is difficult not to tighten up and reinstate excessive verification or review.

Also, some employees either don't want to accept larger responsibility or have become so conditioned over the years that they expect to be told what, where, when, and how to do the job.

Costs. There were significant savings in the Stock and Bond Division, a few of which have been cited.

In the way of out-of-pocket expense, the three-day Managing for Growth Conference costs about $100 per person.

The manpower utilization staff consists of six people with a budget of about $76,000. They spend half their time in the work-itself area and the other half leading and preparing other management training courses.

SUMMARY

We in the Treasury Department feel that the work-itself programs have been profitable to the company and have provided more satisfying jobs for our employees. The managers feel that they have made good progress since the study ended.

It takes much delegation, job redesign, commitment to the concepts, and trust in what people in lower levels can really do, given the opportunity. In Treasury, in this climate created by more attention to better utilization of talent and examination of job content, managers ask themselves more frequently, "What can I do to this clerical job to make it more meaningful to the employee so that his talents are utilized and his efforts are recognized?" "Is this a good second-level assignment?" "Will this assignment really challenge the creativity of this person?"

When the manager accepts this responsibility and is *assigned the task* of giving substance and life to the concepts, it ceases to be a program and becomes part of day-to-day managerial practice.

Appendix B

The Framemen Trial

AMERICAN TELEPHONE AND TELEGRAPH COMPANY
Long Lines Department
Northeastern Area Plant

Project Report
HARRY J. SHEAFFER
Coordinator

November 24, 1967

Appendix B

The Framemen Trial

THIS PROJECT INVOLVING CENTRAL OFFICE FRAMEMEN WAS COORDINATED
by Harry J. Sheaffer, Long Lines Department, Northeastern Area
Plant of the American Telephone and Telegraph Company. He also
wrote this report, which was published on November 24, 1967.

ACKNOWLEDGMENT

Those managers whose cooperation and contributions made this trial
possible were

A. C. Stark, Jr.	Area Plant Manager
Q. I. Peters	Area Staff Supervisor
S. R. Willcoxon	Plant Operating Engineer
R. S. Beck	Division Plant Manager
D. R. Santomenna	District Plant Manager
R. Haufler	Plant Manager
J. E. Ahearn	Plant Manager
M. F. Kleinbard	Staff Supervisor
L. Capolino	Plant Supervisor
R. N. Ford	Management Training Supervisor
G. Nagel	Information Systems Coordinator
G. A. Wetzel	Staff Representative

211

The basic theory of the work-itself concept as a work motivator is best described in Chapter 2, Part A, in the report of the pilot study by Robert N. Ford and Malcolm B. Gillette.

THE PROBLEM

In the Long Lines plant of the New York Private Line Telephone District, 40 men were assigned to perform private line telephone circuit installation work. Prior to the start of this project, the assignment of these 40 men was split between two plant managers' groups. Group 1 was concerned primarily with writing up the equipment cross-connection card from the circuit order, testing the circuit, and turning up the circuit to the customer or the control office.

Group 2 was concerned with performing the actual cross-connection work, conditioning the equipment as indicated, and clearing circuit order troubles. In addition, this group had other responsibilities such as "K" carrier maintenance and the entire job on telephoto circuits (including installation, maintenance, and operation), power maintenance, and other equipment maintenance.

In the installation of a private line telephone circuit, the service order was received by Group 1 and the cross-connection card was prepared. This card was then passed to Group 2, which performed the actual frame work. When the work was completed and the equipment was conditioned, a report to that effect was given to Group 1, which would perform the appropriate tests. If trouble was found on the circuit, it was passed back to Group 2 again for clearance.

The cross-connection groups were assigned to all three tours (days, evenings, and nights), with the majority of the framemen being assigned to the day tour. The men who had longer service generally asked for and were assigned the night and evening tours.

The duties of these framemen consisted primarily of interconnecting equipment and lines in accordance with a configuration specified by a cross-connection card (provided by another group). The actual operations involved identifying one set of connecting terminals on the frame, running two or more wires to another set of terminals on another part of the frame, removing a length of insulation from the end of each wire, wrapping the bare end of the wire around the appropriate terminal, and soldering the connection with an electric soldering iron. One such complete operation is referred to as a "jumper," and there may be any number of jumpers per circuit.

Several salient problems existed in this system:

1. The responsibility for the performance of the overall circuit installation on private line telephone circuits was split between two plant managers, with the problems inherent in such an arrangement.
2. The productivity was informally limited to 21 jumpers per man per tour by mutual agreement among the framemen. It was popular to refer to this controlled productivity as the "bogey established by the phantom chief." Attempts to improve productivity were met head-on with the 21-jumpers-per-man-per-tour standard.
3. The morale in the cross-connection group was not good, to say the least.
4. It was difficult if not impossible for the men to personally identify themselves with the completed job; hence the men took little or no pride in their work. They referred to themselves as "frame apes" and felt that little or no intelligence was required to perform the frame job since a man could learn this job in about one week.
5. It was almost impossible for the supervisor to identify the poor or careless performer since there was no quick and simple way to identify his work.
6. Frame errors were reaching a prohibitive level.
7. The percentage of work completed on schedule was well below acceptable standards.
8. The percentage of circuits rejected on test owing to faulty circuit order work was too high to meet acceptable standards.
9. The supervisors seemed to be spending an inordinate amount of time assigning work to the frame crews and coordinating the activities between the work crews. This resulted in a lack of time to plan ahead, devise new and better methods, and so on.

THE PLAN

At the instigation of the Division plant manager, Long Lines, New York Plant Division, a meeting was held on October 17, 1966, which was attended by all levels of supervision in direct line of authority over the study group from the second-level manager through and including the department head. The area general manager participated part time. In addition, interested staff members from the Long Lines Northeastern Area and Long Lines Headquarters Personnel group attended. Staff members from the general departments of AT&T headed by Dr. R. N.

Ford presented the philosophy behind the work-itself theory as a means of motivating people to work. Professor Frederick Herzberg, a psychologist at Case Western Reserve University on whose ideas the work-itself concept is based, also participated in the meeting. At this meeting it was decided to proceed with the project.

It was generally agreed that no substantial change in the job could be made to incorporate vertical loading unless the groups were reorganized to place the more complex work (testing and other service) in the same group with the cross-connection work. Only when the groups were reorganized would it be possible to make significant changes in the job structure in order to make the work more challenging, interesting, and satisfying. Furthermore, the job then could be so organized as to more readily identify each man's work.

This reorganization could be accomplished by reassigning the frame crews to report to the same plant manager who was responsible for the cross-connection writeup and the circuit testing work. Work teams of two or three men could be organized, depending upon the size and complexity of the installation to be accomplished. Each team could be made responsible for the installation of a particular circuit from writeup (the writeup being done by a special group) through turning it up to the customer, including the clearing of troubles attributable to the installation work.

A list of 13 greenlight items (or privileges) was developed that represented vertical loading of the job. (See Exhibit B-1.)

The following is an explanation of the 13 privileges listed in Exhibit B-1:

1. Perform equipment and transmission work. This will include such items as changing repeater gains, strapping signaling equipment, changing pads, and designating equipment—in general, doing any equipment work required to start a service. Maintenance of this equipment remains with the plant manager of Group 2.
2. Perform overall circuit order testing. This can be classified into three categories: central office testing, STC to STC, and customer to customer. It includes meeting all requirements on the circuit layout record cards for transmission and signaling.
3. Direct the frame wiring. Formerly known as the "whip," this job entails organizing the cross-connection job and "running" the cards as leader of a crew.
4. Represent group at meetings. This would apply to intraoffice,

interoffice, or department meetings, unless it is stipulated that a management person must attend.

5. Act as team leader. This man would be the unofficial "in charge" member of a team. He would be the one to whom those with less experience would look for help and guidance and the one from whom the supervisor would ascertain the status of his crew's workload.

6. Appoint team leader replacement. This is a privilege of team leaders when they must be absent from the job for any reason.

7. Determine work priority. While this is normally a team leader's privilege, it is currently a supervisor's responsibility when heavy workloads require that some jobs take a back seat to others.

8. Negotiate temporary force changes. Varying workloads dictate that we borrow people from one group in the office to another. A man having this privilege in the group that requires help could negotiate with supervisors of other groups to supply his needs.

9. Make first- and second-level management contacts. This would hold true for contacts in either Long Lines or associated companies in New York or out of town. It would be up to the man to determine when this contract should be made.

10. Authorize overtime. This is a team leader's privilege when earned. He would determine the need, inform his boss of his actions, and determine whether the job should be continued by the team or whether overtime cards could be used without impairing job efficiency. This item may not become a reality until the program is well established and the entire installation job is being done on a team basis, but it has merit and would certainly be an incentive to the men, since this privilege would really be a demonstration of faith.

11. Negotiate with customers. A man will earn this privilege when his talk and actions indicate that he will put the Bell System's best foot forward to our customers. It will entail such things as getting releases on existing circuits and turn-ups of new circuits.

12. Issue memos. A man with this privilege will be able to do such things as recognize the need for a change in procedure, come up with an improvement idea, and express it clearly in a written memo which he will sign and distribute to the office (including his boss).

(Text continues on page 220.)

Exhibit B-1

SCHEDULE OF IMPLEMENTATION

GREENLIGHT ITEMS
PLANT SUPERVISOR
DAY TOUR A

NAME	1. Perform Both Eqpt. and Trans. Work	2. C.O. Testing / Perform Overall	3. Direct X-Connection Job	4. Represent Groups at Meetings	5. Act as Team Leader	6. Appoint Team Leader Replacement	7. Determine Work Priority	8. Negotiate Temporary Force Changes	9. Make 1st and 2nd Level Mgmt. Contacts	10. Authorize Overtime	11. Negotiate with Customers	12. Issue Memos	13. Conduct Orientation of New Employees	NOTES
F-1	2-67	10-67	3-67				9-67	9-67	9-67	10-67	3-67	3-67		
F-2	11-66	10-67	11-66											
F-3	11-66	9-67	11-66				5-67			4-67	3-67			
F-4	Yes	Yes	Yes										→	Transferred Out of Grp.
F-5	1-67	3-67	2-67	3-67						3-67	3-67	3-67	→	Transferred Out of Grp.
F-6	3-67	3-67	2-67								3-67		→	Dismissed
F-7	Yes	Yes	Yes										→	To Eve. Tour
F-8	3-67	2-67	2-67	1-67	3-67	1-67	3-67	2-67		1-67	1-67	1-67	→	Transferred Out of Grp.
F-9	10-67	10-67	10-67		10-67		10-67	10-67						
F-10	10-67	10-67	10-67	10-67	10-67	10-67	10-67	10-67		10-67	10-67	10-67		
F-11	1966	1966	1-67	1-67	1-67	1-67	3-67	1966		1966	1-67	1-67	→	Promoted
F-12	Yes	9-67	Yes	3-67	3-67	3-67	9-67	9-67		3-67	3-67	3-67		
F-13	10-67	10-67			10-67									
F-14	9-67	10-67	9-67	10-67	10-67	10-67	10-67			9-67	9-67	10-67		
F-15	10-67	10-67		10-67		10-67	10-67			10-67				
F-16	Yes	10-67	Yes											
F-60	2-67	2-67	3-67	2-67	2-67	2-67	4-67	2-67		3-67	2-67	2-67		
F-61	1966	3-67	1966	3-67	3-67	3-67	3-67	3-67		3-67	3-67			

Exhibit B-1 (continued)

SCHEDULE OF IMPLEMENTATION

DAY TOUR B

NAME	1. Perform Both Eqpt. and Trans. Work	2. C.O. Testing, Perform Overall	3. Direct X-Connection, Job Testing	4. Represent Groups at Meetings	5. Act as Team Leader	6. Appoint Team Leader Replacement	7. Determine Work Priority	8. Negotiate Temporary Force Changes	9. Make 1st and 2nd Level Mgmt. Contacts	10. Authorize Overtime	11. Negotiate with Customers	12. Issue Memos	13. Conduct Orientation of New Empls.	NOTES
F-17										9-67			↑	Transferred Out of Grp.
F-18	Yes	Yes	Yes		12-66								↑	Resigned
F-19		2-67	2-67										↑	Resigned
F-20		2-67	2-67										↑	To W/U 2-67
F-21	Yes		Yes										↑	To PLSO 3-67
F-22		Yes	Yes							10-67				
F-23	9-67	10-67	3-67		12-66						10-67		↑	Mil. Svc.
F-24	Yes	Yes	Yes											
F-25	3-67	3-67	3-67					2-67			2-67	3-67	↑	To SSO-CO 2-5-67
F-26	11-67	11-67	11-67								3-67	3-67	↑	Transferred to Day Tour
F-27	Yes	9-67	Yes		12-66		4-67	4-67		4-67	4-67	4-67		
F-28	Yes	Yes	Yes										↑	To Mil. Svc. 2-67
F-29	Yes	Yes	Yes		12-66								↑	Resigned 8-11-67
F-30		Yes	Yes		1-67			1-67			1-67	1-67	↑	Promoted
F-31		Yes											↑	Resigned
F-32	9-67	10-67	9-67	10-67		10-67	10-67	9-67		10-67	10-67	10-67		
F-33	9-67	10-67	9-67	9-67		9-67	9-67	9-67		9-67	9-67	10-67		
F-34	10-67	10-67	10-67								10-67			
F-35														
F-36	8-67	9-67	8-67	10-67			10-67	10-67		10-67	10-67	10-67		
F-37			9-67				10-67	10-67		10-67	10-67	10-67		
F-38	12-67										12-67		↑	Tfd. to Another Group

Exhibit B-1 (continued)

SCHEDULE OF IMPLEMENTATION

EVENING TOUR

NAME	1. Perform Both Eqpt. and Trans. Work	2. Perform Overall C.O. Testing	3. Direct X-Connection Job	4. Represent Groups at Meetings	5. Act as Team Leader	6. Appoint Team Leader Replacement	7. Determine Work Priority	8. Negotiate Temporary Force Changes	9. Make 1st and 2nd Level Mgmt. Contacts	10. Authorize Overtime	11. Negotiate with Customers	12. Issue Memos	13. Conduct Orientation of New Employees	NOTES
F-39	Yes	Yes												
F-40	Yes	Yes	Yes											Tfd. to Eve. Tour
F-41	Yes	Yes	Yes											Tfd. Out of City
F-42	Yes	Yes	Yes											To Day Tour SSO-CO 2-67
F-43	Yes	Yes	Yes											To Day Tour W/U 2-5-67
F-44	Yes		Yes											
F-45	Yes	Yes	Yes											Tfd. to Another Group
F-46	Yes	Yes												Transferred Out of Grp.
F-47														From Days 2-9-67
F-48														
F-49														
F-50	Yes		Yes											
F-51	Yes		Yes											
F-52	Yes		Yes											

Exhibit B-1 (continued)

SCHEDULE OF IMPLEMENTATION

NIGHT TOUR

NAME	1. Perform Both Eqpt. and Trans. Work	2. Perform Overall C.O. Testing	3. Direct X-Connection Job	4. Represent Groups at Meetings	5. Act as Team Leader	6. Appoint Team Leader Replacement	7. Determine Work Priority	8. Negotiate Temporary Force Changes	9. Make 1st and 2nd Level Mgmt. Contacts	10. Authorize Overtime	11. Negotiate with Customers	12. Issue Memos	13. Conduct Orientation of New Employees	NOTES
F-53	Yes	Yes												
F-54	Yes	Yes											↑	To Eve.
F-55	Yes	Yes												
F-56	Yes	Yes												
F-57	Yes	Yes											↑	To Eve.
F-58	Yes	Yes												
F-59	Yes	Yes											↑	To Eve.

13. Conduct orientation of new employees. This task, now handled by supervisors, would allow the craftsmen to talk about *their* jobs.

Four groups consisting of a total of 45 people, also engaged solely in cross-connection work, were selected as control groups. Their jobs were to be left unchanged, and no change was to be made in the method of performance.

At the same time a measurement plan was developed to compare the performance of the achieving group with that of selected control groups. (See Exhibit B-2.)

So as not to call undue attention to the project, it was agreed that neither the craftsmen nor the first-level supervisors would be informed of the reason for the changes in the job. This was done to keep the work setting as natural as possible and to reduce the possibility of the Hawthorne effect.

INSTRUCTION SHEET

1. *Work units per man-hour.* This should be one figure expressed in hundredths to the second decimal point (for example, 6.78) for the period from the 23rd of the preceding month through the 22nd of the current month. This figure should be computed for the group for all "17M" time *less scheduling time included in the 17M account.* It is important that the scheduling time be lifted out and only the time charged for operation other than scheduling be used to compute this performance figure. The existing practices covering the computation of work-unit performance should be followed in arriving at this figure.

2. *Personal absences.* This figure should be expressed in terms of days absent per man for the group for the month involved. As with all the items, the report period shall be from the 23rd of the preceding month through the 22nd of the current month. Absences of less than four hours should be disregarded. Absences of four hours or more, but less than eight hours, should be counted as one-half day. Absences of a full eight-hour day should be counted as one day.

Only those absences which are chargeable under the plan for computing absence statistics by the Accounting Department should be counted. (See Attachment A directly following the Instruction Sheet.) Those absences for which the codes are shown on Attachment B should be excluded for purposes of this study. For a group of 15 men, 5½ days of absences occurring in that month would be computed as follows:

$$5.5 \div 15 = .366 \text{ (express on the report as .37)}.$$

(*Text continues on page 226.*)

Exhibit B-2

SPECIAL WORK PERFORMANCE STUDY–NORTHEASTERN AREA
PLANT AREA STAFF SUPERVISOR

ACHIEVING GROUP

Period Ending	1966	1967								
ITEM	12-22	1-22	2-22	3-22	4-22	5-22	6-22	7-22	8-22	9-22
1. Work Units per Man Hour		5.78	6.37	5.68	4.07	4.12	4.60	4.87	5.79	5.92
2. Personal Absences		.66	.36	.42	.68	1.0	.42	.29	.937	.257
3. Tardiness		.57	1.30	.66	.25	.38	.27	.15	.206	.229
4. Overtime		49.7	24.5	29.8	24.2	19.3	20.1	26.4	10.9	15.73
5. Percent Work Complete		50	81	104	97.3	99.5	98.	91.	103.8	101.6
6. Patches Due to Uncompleted Circuit Order Work		75	89	32	34	40	23	26	24	19

Exhibit B-2 (continued)

CONTROL GROUP #1

Period Ending	1966	1967								
ITEM	12-22	1-22	2-22	3-22	4-22	5-22	6-22	7-22	8-22	9-22
1. Work Units per Man Hour		6.52	5.48	6.40	7.22	8.76	8.29	7.96	4.79	
2. Personal Absences		.44	0	.54	.20	.00	.00	.80	.10	
3. Tardiness		.25	1.16	.09	.10	.00	.00	.00	.20	
4. Overtime		1.5	2.6	2.2	2.4	4.0	7.0	11.2	0.0	
5. Percent Work Complete		97.4	98.5	97.4	98.0	84.7	96.2	99.0	99.0	
6. Patches Due to Uncompleted Circuit Order Work		18	11	18	10	28	16	5	2	

Exhibit B-2 (continued)

CONTROL GROUP #2

Period Ending	1966	1967								
ITEM	12-22	1-22	2-22	3-33	4-22	5-22	6-22	7-22	8-22	9-22
1. Work Units per Man Hour	4.17	5.24	4.25	4.43	3.91	3.32	5.97	4.02	4.82	
2. Personal Absences	.08	.25	.41	.08	.18	.20	.33	.09	0	
3. Tardiness	.41	.33	.12	.16	.45	.45	.02	.09	.18	
4. Overtime	38.5	7.6	1.0	6.3	7.1	14.5	12.6	7.72	6.63	
5. Percent Work Complete	100	95	78.5	99.0	99.6	98.9	100	100	98	
6. Patches Due to Uncompleted Circuit Order Work	0	—	—	3	6	—	0	0	0	

Exhibit B-2 (continued)

CONTROL GROUP #3

Period Ending	1966	1967									
ITEM	12-22	1-22	2-22	3-22	4-22	5-22	6-22	7-22	8-22	9-22
1. Work Units per Man Hour		2.92	5.69	5.89	3.39	3.43	10.29	9.50	7.30	12.37
2. Personal Absences		0	.25	0	0	0	.43	0	0	.75
3. Tardiness		0	0	0	0	0	0	.14	0	0
4. Overtime		0	4.0	7.1	13.3	15.2	8.2	23.75	0	8.49
5. Percent Work Complete		100	100	100	100	100	100	100	100	100
6. Patches Due to Uncompleted Circuit Order Work		0	0	0	0	0	0	0	0	0

Exhibit B-2 (continued)

CONTROL GROUP #4

Period Ending	1966	1967								
ITEM	12-22	1-22	2-22	3-22	4-22	5-22	6-22	7-22	8-22	9-22
1. Work Units per Man Hour		3.83	1.46	1.70	2.26	4.58		1.84	62.43	
2. Personal Absences		0	.33	0	.03	.16	1.0	.67	.67	
3. Tardiness		.20	.07	.14	.36	.25	.17	.50	.17	
4. Overtime		8.0	3.0	4.0	.6	10.8	19.0	28.41	15.91	
5. Percent Work Complete		97.2	90.5	77.5	60	78.4	90	85	95	
6. Patches Due to Uncompleted Circuit Order Work		0	14	14	9	11	12	12	15	

3. *Tardiness.* Count each incident of tardiness or lateness exceeding seven minutes as one incident. Compute as in Item 2 and express ir hundredths.

4. *Overtime.* Express as clock hours per man per month. Thus 110 hours overtime for a group of 15 men for the month would be computed as follows:

$$110 \div 15 = 7.333 \text{ (express as 7.33 on the report).}$$

5. *Percent work complete.* This item is intended to measure the percentage of circuit order items completed on time as scheduled. Tabulate the total number of circuit order items scheduled for the period of the report. Determine the number of the items scheduled that were *completed on time.* Divide the number of items scheduled into the number of items completed on time and express in percent carried to one point beyond the decimal. Count as completed those items put up on patches on time. If 331 items were scheduled and 317 were completed on time, the computation would be:

$$317 \div 331 = 95.77 \text{ (express as 95.8 percent).}$$

6. *Patches due to uncompleted circuit order work.* Express in terms of the actual *number of items* put up on patches on time, but not wired in during the report period.

For this study to have valid significance, it is essential that the results reported reflect accurately the actual performance of the group. It is obvious that figures for such a small group can be unduly influenced by certain happenings which are beyond the control of the immediate group. Examples of such happenings would be an extended disability or a sudden surge of circuit order work totally unforeseen and unusual. Such happenings should be brought to the personal attention of the study coordinator.

It is planned that the monthly results be telephoned to the coordinator no later than the third working day following the end of the report period.

Questions regarding this study should be directed to the coordinator.

IMPLEMENTING THE PLAN

The organization for the study. On November 14, 1966, the district manager transferred the cross-connection group to the plant manager who had the writeup and testing responsibility, thus placing the respon-

(Text continues on page 234.)

Attachment A

CODES INCLUDED IN ABSENCE STATISTICS

Code Paid	Code Unpaid	Included As a Scheduled Day	Including Absence	Disability and Other	
PS	AS	X	X		Sickness—1 to 7 full calendar days and first partial day.
PP	AP	X	X		Other reasons—1 to 7 full calendar days and first partial day for the following reasons: Illness of others in family. Care of children, illness of members of family. Failure of transportation under conditions not severe enough in the judgment of management to warrant exclusion from incidental absence. No report.
PG	AG	X		X	Other reasons—8th full day through 30th calendar day (reasons as above for PP, AP) (including partial day).
PC	AC	X		X	Sickness—8th full day through 30th calendar day (not covered by the benefit plan).
PJ	AJ	X	X		Off-duty accident—1 to 7 full calendar days.

Attachment A (continued)

Paid Code	Unpaid Code	Included As a Scheduled Day	Including Absence	Disability and Other	
PG	AQ	X		X	Off-duty accident—8th full day through 30th calendar day (not covered by the benefit plan).
DA	—	X		X	Accident disability-on-the-job—1st full day for 52 weeks.
DG	—	X		X	Holiday code—last disability day—off-duty accident.
DH	—	X		X	Sickness disability—relapse—1 to 7 days—hospitalized.
DK	—	X		X	Sickness disability—off-duty accident—8 to 30 days.
DN	—	X		X	Sickness disability—relapse—hospitalized—off-duty accident 1 to 7 days.
DO	—	X		X	Other benefits.
DQ	—	X		X	Sickness disability—off-duty accident—over 30 days.
DR	—	X		X	Sickness disability—relapse—1 to 7 days.
DS	—	X		X	Sickness disability—8th full day—30 calendar days.
DW	—	X		X	Sickness disability—over 30 calendar days.
DX	—	X		X	Holiday code—last day of disability (no accident).
DY	—	X		X	Sickness disability—relapse—off-duty accident—1 to 7 days.

Attachment B

Codes Excluded from Absence Statistics

Paid	Code Unpaid	Included As a Scheduled Day	
PV	—	X	Vacation.
—	AV	X	Extended vacation.
PX	—	X	Time off as compensation for holiday in employee's vacation week.
PM	AM	X	Peacetime military duty.

Union Activities

Paid	Code Unpaid	Included As a Scheduled Day	
—	AB	X	Local business—form D2.
—	AF	X	National business—form D1
	AI	X	Incidental absence—other than union representative.
—	AY	X	Leave of absence—local business—form D2.
—	AZ	X	Leave of absence—national business—form D1.
PK	—	X	Meeting with management—form U319.
PO	AO	X	Absence not to exceed one month for following reasons:

Paid	Code Unpaid	Included As a Scheduled Day	
			Death in family.
			Attending funeral.
			Jury duty.
			Court appearance.
			Visit to medical department.
			Own marriage.
			Quarantine.
			Extended transportation failure.
			Any absence other than illness for which advance notice has been given or time off granted, where force conditions permit, for personal undertakings.
PD	AD	X	Sickness over 30 days (not covered by the benefit plan).
CX	—	X	Compensating time off (in lieu of payment for extra time worked).
HX	—	X	Holiday excused.
—	NX	—	Not scheduled.
TA	—	X	Time absent—temporary work location hours are less than home location hours.
—	NE	—	Not employed.
PN	AN	X	Off-duty accident over 30 days—not covered by benefit plan.
DB	—	X	On-the-job accident disability—over 30 days not covered by the benefit plan.

Exhibit B-3

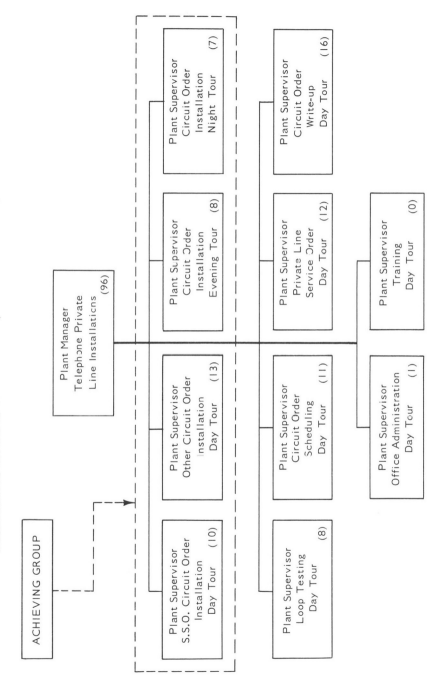

ASSIGNMENTS AFTER REORGANIZATION (EFFECTIVE 11-14-66)

ACHIEVING GROUP

Plant Manager
Telephone Private
Line Installations (96)

Plant Supervisor
S.S.O. Circuit Order
Installation
Day Tour (10)

Plant Supervisor
Other Circuit Order
Installation
Day Tour (13)

Plant Supervisor
Circuit Order
Installation
Evening Tour (8)

Plant Supervisor
Circuit Order
Installation
Night Tour (7)

Plant Supervisor
Loop Testing
Day Tour (8)

Plant Supervisor
Circuit Order
Scheduling
Day Tour (11)

Plant Supervisor
Private Line
Service Order
Day Tour (12)

Plant Supervisor
Circuit Order
Write-up
Day Tour (16)

Plant Supervisor
Office Administration
Day Tour (1)

Plant Supervisor
Training
Day Tour (0)

Exhibit B-3 (continued)

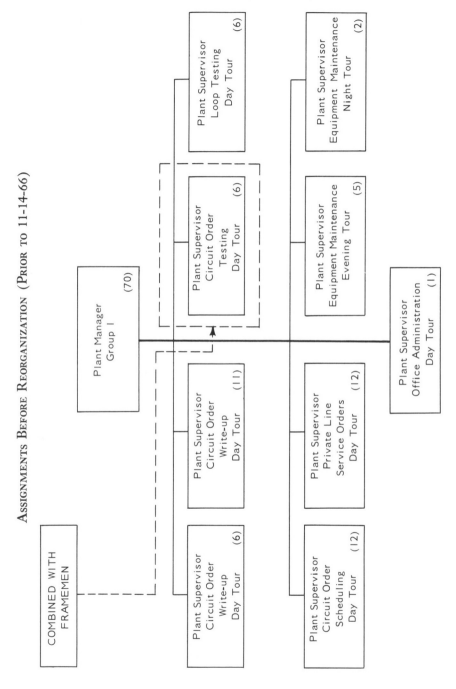

ASSIGNMENTS BEFORE REORGANIZATION (PRIOR TO 11-14-66)

Exhibit B-3 (continued)

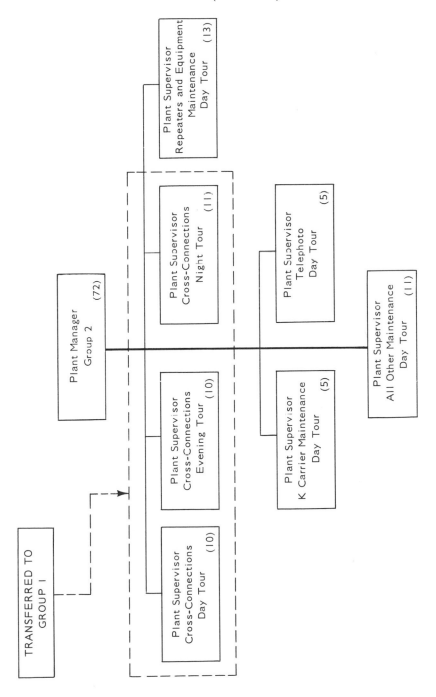

sibility for the entire circuit installation under one plant manager. (See the "before" and "after" charts contained in Exhibit B-3.)

There were eight specific groups involved in the study. The groups retained their natural identity by remaining in separate and distinct supervisory units. Four of these groups were designated as achieving groups, and the other four were designated as control groups. All were located in New York City. No control groups were selected outside of New York City since no groups existed anywhere else whose duties were closely comparable to those of the achieving group for any significant period of time.

I. Achieving groups

2 Supervisory groups—day tour	23
1 Supervisory group—evening tour	8
1 Supervisory group—night tour	7
Total	38*

II. Control groups

No. 1—N.Y. 4 Switching and maintenance office	22
No. 2—N.Y. 7 Message and switching office	7
No. 3—N.Y. 7 Facilities office	6
No. 4—N.Y. 1A Switchboard	10
Total	45

SETTING THE CLIMATE

Upper management. Upper management had participated in the exploratory and planning stages of the project. It was generally understood that a noticeable decline in results could occur in the early stages of the trial, but it was expected that this decline would be moderate and tolerable. Nevertheless, local managers were admonished to take whatever corrective measures were necessary, without regard for the trial, should this decline reach a point where it dangerously affected our ability to furnish acceptable service to the customer.

First-line management. Since the plant manager's group had been reorganized to absorb the frame crews, a natural need arose to conduct

*By January 1967, this group increased to 40 (25 on day tour).

a meeting with all his first-level supervisors to discuss the reallocation of responsibilities and duties between supervisors' groups. The plant manager used this opportunity to conduct a greenlight or creative thinking session similar to the one conducted in the first project meeting. Interestingly enough, a list of items almost identical to the one suggested in the first project meeting was developed.

Since the first-line supervisors were personally involved in the formulation of the plan, little or no conditioning was required to motivate them to implement the plan. The supervisors showed some concern as to whether the plant manager would be permitted by his boss and upper management to operate under the plan the group had developed. *The first-line supervisors were not informed that a study was being conducted.*

Employee level. Each supervisor in the achieving group discussed the new organization and method of procedure with his employees. He informed them that they were going to be assigned to teams of two or three men depending on the size of the installation to be accomplished. One member of the team would be designated as the team leader and would be responsible for the installation of the entire circuit from receipt of the writeup through to turning up the circuit to the customer.

In addition, they were told that various privileges would be made available to them as they demonstrated their capability of accepting greater responsibility. They were not made aware of the specific enrichment items that were available to them. However, as each man became qualified for a certain privilege, it was specifically granted by the supervisor. As the project progressed, the men became aware of the various privileges available. In this way, while a list was available to management (see Exhibit B-1), there was no limit to the items that could be added at a later date. Furthermore, this method tended to avoid the implication that there was no more to be gained once a man had been granted all the privileges on the list.

The men were told that they would be trained to handle additional duties. Some framemen had no training in testing and some testers had no training in running cross-connections, hence a substantial amount of cross-training had to be accomplished.

INTRODUCTION OF VERTICAL JOB LOADING FOR THE ACHIEVING GROUP

The following enrichment items were introduced to activate the suggested motivation:

Item	*Motivator Involved*
1. Perform both equipment and transmission work	Growth and learning
2. Perform overall circuit testing	Growth and learning
3. Direct cross-connection job	Responsibility, achievement, and recognition
4. Represent groups at meetings	Responsibility and recognition
5. Act as team leader	Responsibility, growth, and advancement
6. Appoint team leader replacement	Responsibility
7. Determine work priority	Responsibility
8. Negotiate temporary force changes	Responsibility
9. Make first-level and second-level management contacts	Recognition
10. Authorize overtime	Responsibility and achievement
11. Negotiate with customers for circuit releases	Responsibility, growth, and learning
12. Issue memos	Achievement, responsibility, and recognition
13. Conduct orientation of new employees and tours of visitors	Recognition and personal achievement

Teams were assigned according to the capabilities of the individuals available. Those men who possessed at least minimal skills were assigned to teams immediately. Those who required training received the training on the job. Some of the training was performed by the supervisor and some was accomplished on the job through the "buddy system." As other men became qualified they were assigned to teams and granted certain privileges. (Exhibit B-1 shows the rate of implementation by individual names.)

The team leader was permitted to select a particular circuit and to use his own judgment with respect to priority as based on the due dates of the service.

The team members decided how they were going to proceed and made

.e necessary arrangements. If a working circuit was involved, the men made arrangements with the customer for release of the circuit. They identified the location of the equipment terminals on the frame and ran the appropriate cross-connections. They conditioned the equipment as necessary—adjusting gains, changing repeater coil strappings, plugging in the appropriate pads, installing proper options on the equipment, and so on.

Without any further direction from supervision, the men on the team made the appropriate tests within the office and corrected any trouble. If their office *was* the designated control office, they would perform the overall tests on the circuit and turn up the circuit to the customer. If their office was *not* the designated overall control office, the team would report completion of the work to the designated control office and participate in the overall tests.

As individuals became qualified they would be assigned as team leaders. Existing team leaders helped in the selection of new leaders. If a leader needed additional help for a particular installation, he was free to negotiate with another team leader for the loan of a man. The team leader was free to discuss his plans or problems with the supervisor (first level) or the plant manager (second level) at his own discretion. In coordinating activities within the office and establishing local methods, the team leader was permitted to issue office memos, signed by himself. The team leader also conducted tours of the office in the orientation of new employees and was assigned as the tour guide to escort outside visitors through the office.

These points are by no means a complete résumé of the action taken by the supervisors to enrich the workers' jobs. Many day-to-day situations arose which presented the supervisor with the opportunity to allow the employee to use his own judgment and creativity. As the individual supervisors became more and more adept at implementing the work-itself philosophy, more frequent advantage was taken of these opportunities.

Because of opposing precedent dealing with the "equalization of overtime" and the company's contractual obligation associated therewith, Item 10 of the 13 enrichment items (authorize overtime) was never implemented.

The Measures of Success or Failure

As was the case in similar studies in other departments, management wanted workers to feel better on the job. To measure this, a job satisfaction questionnaire was administered. (See Exhibit B-4.)

(Text continues on page 248.)

Exhibit B-4

Raw Scores
"Reactions to Your Job"
Questionnaire
Long Lines Framemen

BEFORE

Achieving Group Completed Questionnaires	Control Group	Uncommitted
41-1	64-1	80-1
34-1	62-2	49-1
32-1	61-1	48-1
27-1	57-1	44-1
23-1	56-1	41-1
21-1	52-3	40-1
	48-1	38-4
Supervisory Interview	47-1	37-1
73-1	46-2	36-1
70-1	45-1	35-3
67-1	44-1	34-1
63-1	43-2	32-2
62-1	41-2	31-1
61-1	40-1	28-1
60-1	39-2	27-1
58-1	38-1	26-1
56-1	37-1	25-3
55-1	36-1	23-1
53-1	35-1	22-1
51-1	34-1	21-1
44-2	33-1	20-1
43-2	31-2	16-1
39-1		15-2
34-1		14-1
33-1		
32-1		
30-1		
27-1		
25-1		
18-1		

Exhibit B-4 (continued)

AFTER

Achieving Group	Control Group	Uncommitted
42-2	55-1	58-1
39-1	54-1	57-1
37-2	51-1	53-1
32-1	49-2	49-1
23-1	46-1	42-1
21-1	44-2	38-2
18-1	43-3	37-1
	39-3	35-1
	38-1	32-2
	37-1	24-2
	34-1	16-1
	30-2	10-1
	18-1	
	13-1	

NOTE: Figures in left columns are scores; figures in right columns are numbers of people who achieved them.

Exhibit B-4 (continued)

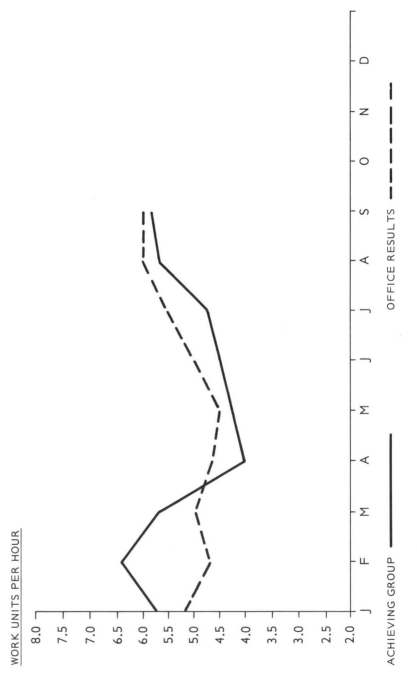

Exhibit B-4 (continued)

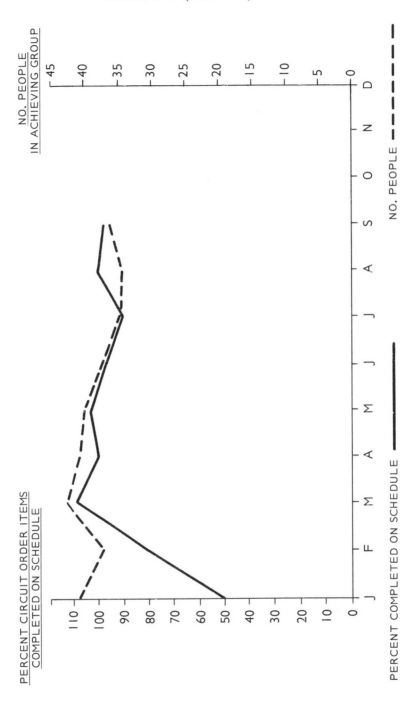

COMPLETION AND FORCE

Exhibit B-4 (continued)

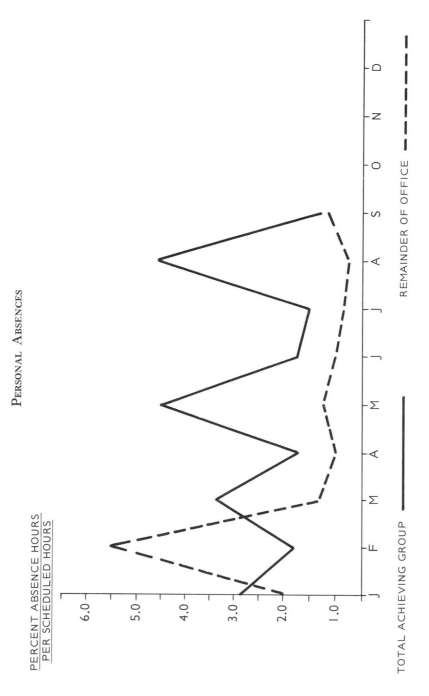

PERSONAL ABSENCES

Exhibit B-4 (continued)

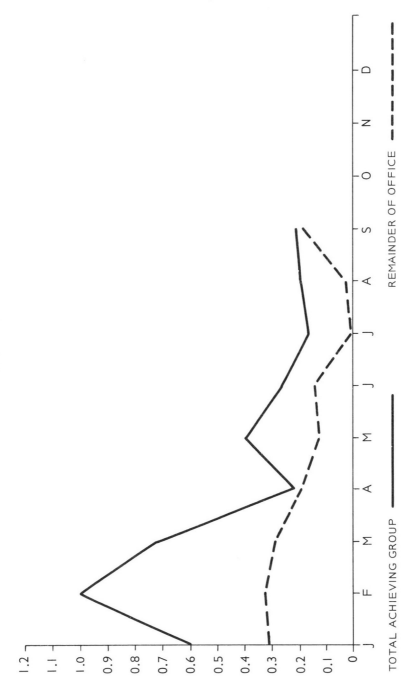

Exhibit B-4 (continued)

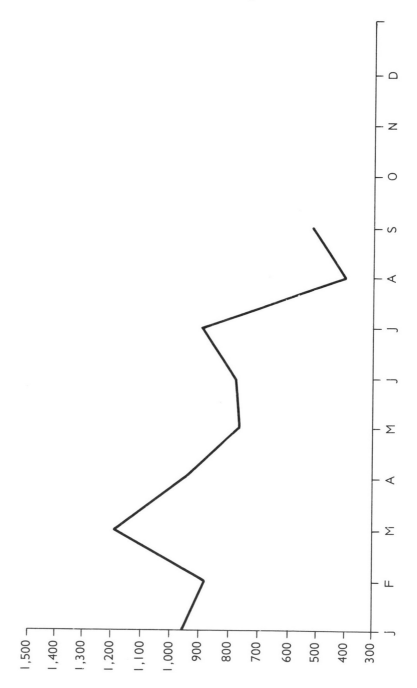

Exhibit B-4 (continued)

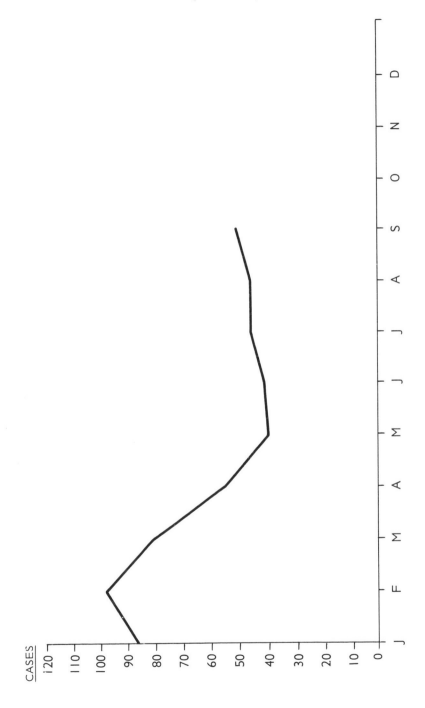

Exhibit B-4 (continued)

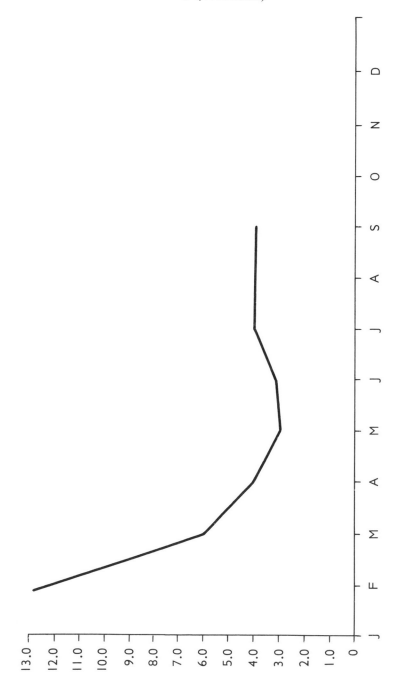

Exhibit B-4 (continued)

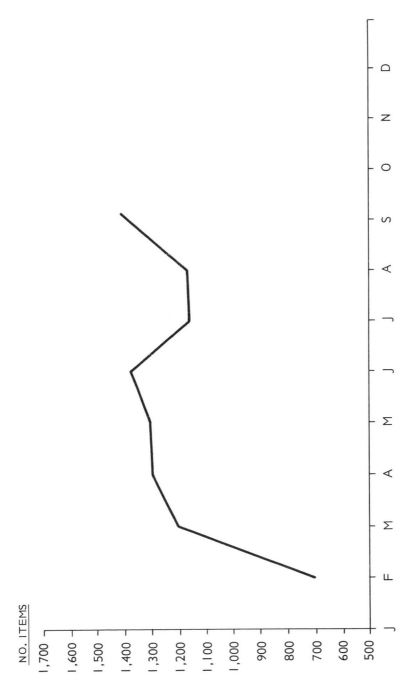

There were no formal work indexes already in existence which covered exclusively work groups of this nature. Therefore, a special work performance measurement plan was developed specifically for this project. The components measured were work units per man-hour, percentage of work completed on schedule, and circuit patches required because of uncompleted circuit order work. (See Exhibit B-2.)

Other measures covered changes in personal absences, tardiness, and overtime worked.

THE RESULTS

"Reactions to Your Job" opinion questionnaire. Because of some adverse union reactions to similar efforts by management, it was decided to advise the local union leaders of the plan to administer the "Reactions to Your Job" questionnaire. They were not told of the project or of the real reason for administering the questionnaire. The union actively opposed the plan.

Nevertheless, management proceeded to administer the questionnaire. The possible score ranged from 0 to 80, with 80 being the top score. Only 6 of the 38 workers in the achieving group completed the questionnaire, and the scores ranged from 21 to 41. An additional 24 workers were interviewed by their supervisors, who then completed the questionnaire on the basis of the interviews. These scores ranged from 18 to 73.

Of the 45 members in the control groups, 30 workers completed the questionnaire. Their scores ranged from 31 to 64.

Thirty-three other workers who were uncommitted to the project completed questionnaires, with scores ranging from 14 to 80. (There was one score of 80 in this group, and the next highest was 49. The effective range could therefore be interpreted to be from 14 to 49.) Exhibit B-4 shows a breakdown of these scores.

At the close of the project, the questionnaire was again administered to the achieving and control groups. No advance notice was given to the union leadership. However, once the test was under way, at least one steward was heard telling the workers not to complete the questionnaire.

Of the 35 men in the achieving group, 9 completed the questionnaire. Their scores ranged from 18 to 42. Of the 45 men in the control groups, 21 completed the questionnaire with scores ranging from 13 to 55. In addition, 15 employees uncommitted to the project completed the questionnaire. Their scores ranged from 10 to 58. A final breakdown of these actual scores is also shown in Exhibit B-4.

Technical results. The work units per man-hour for the achieving group showed some significant trends. They went from a high of 6.37

in January to a low of 4.12 in April. After that point the results showed a fairly steady upward trend through the close of the project. It should be noted that the circuit order scheduling job was transferred from this group to a centralized group in Cincinnati, Ohio, in March 1967 with a corresponding loss of work units. It should also be noted that a significant amount of production time was lost to training in the early stages of the project to prepare the workers to accept their broader responsibilities.

The percentage of work completed on schedule showed no significant trend in the control groups. However, there was a significant surge during the first two months in the achieving group, and this gain was sustained throughout the period of the study. The achieving group was ahead of schedule in March, August, and September. This did not occur in the control groups.

The results for the patches owing to uncompleted circuit order work criterion were erratic for both the achieving and control groups. However, both groups showed an overall favorable trend.

Other quantitative results. Personal absences showed no significant change during the period of the study for either the achieving or control groups. As a matter of fact, the results of the achieving group were even less favorable than those of the remainder of the plant manager's office to which the achieving group is assigned.

Tardiness, while showing an improvement for the achieving group during the course of the study, could not keep pace with the standard of the remainder of the office. The control groups were generally as good as or better than the achieving group.

Overtime for the achieving group showed a general decline during the period of the study. In the control groups, the overtime showed a general increase. In the achieving group, there had been a history of overtime almost directly corresponding to the number of circuit order items completed. During the period of the study, although the number of employees in the group was reduced from 40 in January to 35 in September, overtime hours declined and the number of items completed generally increased.

Local measurements. In addition to the measured items contained in the original plan, the plant manager recorded results in two other areas: circuit order items completed and frame errors.

The number of circuit order items completed generally increased during the course of the study. While each circuit order item varies as to the number of operations required to complete it, over a broad base the items are believed to be equalized to the extent that a measurement such as this is accepted as reasonably valid.

Frame errors dropped from a high of 90 in February to a low of

36 in May. Since May the trend has been slightly upward, but it has not approached the February level. However, the number of circuit order items completed has also increased substantially.

Some subjective results. The supervisors in the project have volunteered these important observations or impressions of the project.

1. Employees in nearby groups which were not involved in the project liked what they saw happening in this group and wanted to be transferred to it.

2. Development of the employees is being accelerated, since they now have a sense of achievement and are motivated to do more. To do more they must learn how, and pressure is generated for the opportunity to learn.

3. The management employees in the achievement group feel that they have much more time to actually manage the overall job since they no longer give detailed direction to each of their people. Furthermore, they have time available to evaluate job methods and procedures and to develop better ways of doing the job.

4. Now the managers can tell almost minute by minute the status of a particular circuit installation, since one crew completes the circuit from beginning to end. This gives management a feeling of having more *real* control over the job even though there is less *detail* control over the people.

5. The work-itself concept was made effective only for that part of the achievement group that was assigned to the day tour. There are various reasons why it could not be put into effect on the night tour. Many of the greenlight items just aren't assignable to the night tour because of the nature of the job. For example, overall testing of the circuit cannot be done because other offices are not covered; conducting tours for visitors cannot be done because visitors are not admitted during the off tours; the older, longer-service people on these tours resist accepting the privilege items; and so on.

   The fact that a part of the achievement group (probably the 14 assigned to the off tours out of 40 in the achievement group) has not been indoctrinated and motivated causes a further distortion in the quantitative results, particularly in attendance and tardiness.

6. While this plan was not designed to enrich the supervisor's job, it was evident that enrichment was a favorable byproduct. The supervisor was indoctrinated with the notion that it is not

the supervisor's job to see that the man does his job right—that's the man's job; the supervisor's job is to see that the man knows what to do and how to do it and that he has the tools to do it. Operating under this theory, the supervisor found that he had more time to plan ahead, devise new methods, and counsel with his people.

7. The plant manager in charge of the achieving group stated that whether or not the work-itself philosophy is adopted by the company, he is going to continue to use it in his group. He said, "I have to. I can't afford to be without it."

How the men view their new jobs. In view of the limited participation in completing the questionnaire, there are no truly scientific facts available to substantiate any change in the feelings of the workers. However, there are certain indications that the men are experiencing a greater satisfaction in their new jobs.

1. In the achieving group 15.8 percent (6 out of 38) of the men completed the questionnaire at the beginning of the project. At the conclusion of the project 25.7 percent (9 out of 35) of the men completed the questionnaire. There was no significant change in the range of points scored. By comparison, in the control groups 66.6 percent (30 out of 45) of the men completed the questionnaires at the start of the study. At the close of the study 46.6 percent (21 out of 45) of the men completed the questionnaire. The range of scores dropped about 10 points for this group during the period of the study.

2. Perhaps one of the most meaningful observations is the fact that no formal union grievances were received from this group during the entire period of the study. Prior to the project, grievances averaged about one each week.

3. The 21-jumpers-per-man-per-tour quota virtually disappeared on the day tour and was not replaced with any other detectable quota.

4. The employees who were not fully trained were constantly pressuring supervision to give them the opportunity to qualify for greater responsibility.

5. Before the start of the project, supervisors always coordinated activities between the tours. Since the project began, the men themselves have coordinated the work between tours.

6. There is no more waiting around for an assignment from the supervisor, even at the beginning of the tour. The men now

come in, select the circuit they want to work on, and proceed to complete the job.

7. Employees not in the achieving group are requesting to be assigned to that group.

8. It used to be unusual for the framemen to engage in shop-talk during their moments of leisure. Now they are frequently heard discussing their work and exchanging experiences in a way that reflects a sense of proprietorship. Terms like "my circuit" and "my customer" are heard more often.

9. The men take more care to do the work right the first time now that they have to clear their own troubles. In addition, there is greater satisfaction in having the circuit meet the tests on the first attempt.

There are other pertinent indicators, among them these three points:

1. There was a significant reduction in trouble reports in the first 30 days after installation. This printout covers all such troubles reported during the four weeks preceding the date of the report. The number of such troubles reported diminished from 56 reported on April 24 to 33 reported on May 5 to 4 reported on June 9. These figures represent troubles reported for the entire circuit. On the June 9 report, only one could be connected even remotely with this cross-connection group. Subsequent to June 9, 4 to 10 troubles were reported for each 30-day period.

2. The greenlight items were never effectively implemented in the night and evening tours. However, the groups on these tours are now doing the intraoffice testing which they previously had not done. And, as a matter of interest, they still produced the 21 jumpers per man per tour.

3. While the quantitative results charts generally show measurements for the period January through September, these jobs were not fully loaded until late February or early March. This was due in part to the reorganization, in part to the extensive training that had to be accomplished, and surely in part to the reluctance of supervisors to move too fast.

SUMMARY

The results of this study can be generally summarized in four broad categories.

1. *Technical results.* Frame errors have declined; substantially more work is being completed on schedule; there is much better job continuity between tours; and there is substantial evidence of improved quality on new circuit installations.
2. *The workers.* Employees feel that their abilities are being recognized and utilized, making their job more interesting and giving them a greater sense of real accomplishment. Their development is being accelerated, since they have felt a sense of achievement and are motivated to do more. The desire to learn generates pressure to be given the opportunity to learn. This obviously accelerates personal development. Morale is much higher and the jumper quota system has been virtually eliminated on the day tour.
3. *Managers.* The supervisors feel that they have more time to manage the overall job now that they do not give detailed direction to each of their people. Furthermore, they have time to evaluate job methods and procedures and to develop better ways of doing the job. Now they can tell the status of a particular circuit installation almost minute by minute because one crew completes the circuit from beginning to end. The result is that the supervisors feel that their own jobs have been enriched.
4. *The customer.* It is difficult to define the customer in this case since the "customer" most directly involved is the testroom service group. The members of this group feel that they are now getting a much better product. Some measure of the "real paying customers" feeling is reflected in the noticeable reduction in trouble reports in the first 30 days after installation.

The measurements employed in this project were not sufficiently sophisticated to determine with any degree of validity the dollar gains or losses resulting from this approach. However, it is evident that (1) morale in the day tour of the achieving group has changed from one of the lowest to one of the highest in the New York Division and (2) the workers are much more receptive to supervision. The latter result, particularly, appears to be the product of making controls more job-oriented than individual-oriented. This supports the premise of this study that, for supervision to be effective, it must start with the basic concept that the supervisor is in charge of work, not people. When work content is not satisfactory, people will react badly to it. The supervisor cannot do as much to change people as he can to change work.

Implementation of the enrichment items was not fully accomplished. During the course of the entire study, 56 separate individuals were assigned to the achieving group at one time or another and were exposed to job enrichment. At the close of the study 35 of these same people were still in the achieving group. The following table shows the number of people exposed and the degree to which privileges have been granted to them.

Percent of Privileges Granted	No. of People Assigned at Close of Study	Total Exposed
100 percent	6	8
50 percent to 99 percent	8	15
25 percent to 49 percent	5	9
24 percent or less	16	24
	35	56

It is significant that, in spite of the modest degree of implementation, substantial gains were realized.

CONCLUSIONS

The work-itself concept includes more than just changing the job itself. The job may have been so simplified as to be stripped of most of its challenging and satisfying aspects. Consequently, to fit the worker to the job, it was necessary to ignore many of his natural talents and deny him the opportunity to "think" in the performance of the tasks. Now, in an attempt to provide employee satisfaction, we begin to "bribe" him with more pay, better working conditions, and a host of other maintenance items. In effect, he is not being paid for what he does; he is being paid for what he is not allowed to do.

As in the framemen example, the more challenging part of the job may even have been transferred to another group. To load the job vertically it was therefore necessary to reorganize in order to place the more satisfying operations back into the framemen's hands. Only then could the job be "put back together."

In certain cases, before the worker can be given the added responsibility, he must be trained in the new aspects of his job and must demonstrate his capability.

It was observed that for an approach such as this to be effective, a real change—a two-way exchange—has to take place at the first-line supervisor/craftsman interface. It is not enough for the supervisor just to *tell* the craftsman that he has more responsibility and the freedom to exercise it; the craftsman must in fact accept and assume that responsibility. In addition, the supervisor must continually "feed" the system by demonstrating his support in his day-to-day contacts with his employees. He must be constantly aware that, if his behavior contradicts his words, his actions will speak so loudly that others will not hear what he is saying. He must in fact let the craftsmen exercise their own judgment.

This same type of support must extend upward through several levels of management. Just how high this philosophy must penetrate is difficult to determine. What is obvious, however, is that it must go high enough to avoid giving the worker the impression that this is just another approach to human relations.

In any event, the worker must be convinced that he *has* a more responsible job, that he is being held personally accountable, and that his efforts are sincerely recognized.

This study supports Herzberg's theory that there are great gains to be realized by giving the employee challenging work assignments and by holding him responsible for performing his job competently and completely. So far as the maintenance items are concerned, good working conditions, good company policies, good administration, and good supervision are necessary and expected by the employees. It is just as necessary that wages and benefit programs be competitive with other industries. In other words, they must be maintained in the "good pay" range in order that we may attract and hold the number of qualified employees needed in our business. But these maintenance items alone are not sufficient to assure good production over an extended period of time.

The real motivators of improved employee performance and job satisfaction the employee finds in being responsible for his job, in the sense of achievement gained in doing the job, and in the recognition and opportunities for advancement inherent in good work performance.

The employee who found the frameman's job challenging when he was first employed may find it a monotonous chore after he has become familiar with it. From this trial it seems apparent that the job can and should be restructured along the lines developed for the achieving group in this study so that the work can be improved and made more meaningful for the employee.

The very nature of Long Lines—the growing complexities of the hardware and the rapid growth of the business—seems to make this organization an ideal setting for large-scale use of the work-itself approach.

It may very well be that some jobs cannot be enriched and that some employees cannot be motivated by this approach. For any one of a number of reasons, some employees have reached a point of frustration in their work where they resist accepting additional responsibility. They just want to be told what to do and be left alone to do it at their own pace. To quote Dr. Herzberg, "Resurrection is much more difficult than giving birth." Consequently, it may be even more important to guard against further fractionalizing of jobs to the point where all the real challenges and responsibilities are removed.

THE FUTURE

This report marks the end of the formal study. Many people are asking—and rightly so—"Where do we go from here?"

The plant manager of the achieving group states that he visualizes even greater possibilities in this approach. His organization consists of five functional units. As each unit becomes proficient in its particular functional responsibilities, his plan is to further combine operations in these four steps.

Step 1. Combine the X-connection group and the circuit order testing group. This has been accomplished in the work-itself project.

Step 2. In the future, further combine the circuit order writeup group with the new group formed in Step 1.

Step 3. Combine the private line service order (SSO) group with the loop-testing group.

Step 4. Combine both groups formed by the accomplishment of Step 2 and Step 3 to create an organization in which the entire work responsibility and performance for this group is divided vertically. Each work unit or team would perform the entire job from receiving the circuit order (or service order) to turning up the circuit for service.

This concept appears to approach the ultimate in job enrichment for this group.

Only Step 1 of this plan has been accomplished as of this writing. Although the timetable for subsequent steps has not been established, it is clear that this is a time-consuming process. As one manager put it, "It took ten years for these men to evolve into frame apes. We cannot hope to completely reverse the process in six months."

In this trial, we reached a critical decision point. We had the choice of further fractionalizing the framemen's job in an attempt to create greater efficiency or of putting the job back together again to create a more challenging assignment, trusting that the men's natural desire to achieve would provide the motivation for greater productivity. Our strategy for job enrichment was the latter.

Index

Index

A

absence control, 35
absence statistics, in framemen trials, 227-230, 242-243
achievement:
  human needs and, 24
  job satisfaction and, 23-24
  motivation and, 148
  turnover and, 34-35
alienation, of employees, 91
American Psychological Association, 133
American Telephone and Telegraph Co., 16, 18
  framemen trial, Long Lines Dept., 211-256
  Treasury Dept. trials, 20-43, 203-208
animal needs, motivation and, 26
appraisal form, work-itself project, 82-83
Argyris, Chris, 133
Armstrong, G. N., 22 n.
AT&T, see American Telephone and Telegraph Company
attitude, job, 38-39, 124-125
see also job attitude
attitude questionnaire, 124

B

behavior:
  selective or differential reinforcement in, 134
  in work-itself concept, 133-136
Bell Telephone System, 13, 45
  operating companies of, 17
  resignations and dismissals in, 14
  work problems in, 15-16
  see also American Telephone and Telegraph Company
Between Parent and Child (Ginnott), 138
black employee, job satisfaction for, 192-193
brainstorming, 141-142
  see also greenlighting
"brass," problem of, 158-160
Brayfield, A. H., 133
broadside approach, vs. deskside, 175
Brown, Howard, 16
business, in work-itself concept, 115
business office supervisor (BOS), service representative and, 63-64

About the Author

ROBERT N. FORD is personnel director—manpower utilization, American Telephone and Telegraph Company. This is a new function in the Bell System, encompassing studies of the utilization of personnel and advice and training in this field. Dr. Ford has also been responsible for the training of college recruiters and for studies of the effectiveness of recruiting at AT&T.

Before coming to the Bell System in 1947, he was a study director with the Research Branch of the Information and Education Division of the War Department during World War II. He received his Ph.D. from the University of Pittsburgh in 1940 in the field of social psychology, and he taught sociology at the University of Kentucky, the University of Alabama, Mississippi State University, and Vanderbilt University before joining government and later industry in full-time research jobs.